YOUR
ECONOMIC DESTINY

Jeff Mendenhall

"You've probably thought to yourself at times, 'I wish I knew then what I know now.' That's exactly how you'll feel while reading this book. As Americans we're never taught in school how to properly manage our money. This book rights that wrong and provides hope that it's never too late to be set free from your financial worries. Jeff Mendenhall's message is clear: There are steps you can take to find financial peace and overflowing abundance, even when the world's financial system is broken."

~Pastor Philip Helmintoller, International Prayer Partners

Your Economic Destiny
by Jeff Mendenhall
Copyright © 2011 TX 7-259-304 by Jeffrey A. Mendenhall

17505 W. Catawba Avenue, Suite 140
Cornelius, NC 28031
www.YourEconomicDestiny.org

International Standard Book Number: 978-0-615-45899-1

For more information on bulk order discounts or to request Jeff Mendenhall to speak to your organization, please call EDI Press at 888-418-2397, email info@youreconomicdestiny.org, or write to: Economic Destiny Institute, 516-D River Hwy Suite 143, Mooresville, NC 28117.

All Scripture quotations, unless otherwise indicated, are from the New King James Version of the Bible. Used by permission.

Printed in the United States of America.

TABLE OF CONTENTS

DEDICATION

The messages contained within these pages are

a result of faith, patience, and sacrificial love for "all."

I DEDICATE THIS BOOK

to those who hear the call of stewardship,

take action, and begin impacting the lives of others.

And to those who are willing to leave a legacy of Liberty,

Honor, and Truth to the generations who will

follow wherever you lead.

ACKNOWLEDGEMENTS

SPECIAL THANKS TO...

EVERYONE whose advice, support, and encouragement made this book possible:

My loving wife, CARRIE, for never losing hope. I'll forever be grateful for your unwavering, childlike faith and encouragement as I wrote this book.

My mother, JOYCE, who gave her time, editorial skills, and faithful prayers.

JIM BUCHAN, my editor, for his editorial expertise and willingness to take on a new author's project. This book would never have been published without your help and Biblical insights.

A special thank you to the FINANCIAL MENTORS who raised key questions that brought needed clarity to the final structure of the work.

DYLAN WHEELER for his excellence in creative design and diligent attention to detail.

DANA ZONDORY for her patience, talent, and creative input.

And to EVERYONE who has touched my life. I have learned something of value from each one of you, and the seeds you've planted in me will continue to grow andimpact the lives of countless others. I pray you will be greatly rewarded.

NOT JUST ANOTHER
FINANCE BOOK

H AVE YOU EVER FELT LIKE the cards are stacked against you when it comes to your financial future? Then this book is for you!

The principles described in this book will provide you with a time-tested, common-sense approach to managing your money. Along with the ageless wisdom of Scripture, I share today's most innovative and ground-breaking tools for eliminating debt and building long-term wealth.

The 7 keys are remarkably simple, and I guarantee they won't weigh you down with a boatload of additional items for your "To Do" list. In fact, my goal is to *remove* your burdens instead of add to them. *I want to transform your relationship with money forever!*

If you're like most people, you're tired of chasing fool's gold. You want the real thing! And you've had enough of financial quick-fixes that end up only *increasing* your long-term bondage to debt and prevent you from building a solid financial future. You want relief that *lasts*.

Regardless of how good or how bad your current financial situation may be, the 7 keys and the practical tools discussed in this book are just what you need to start creating economic health for you and your loved ones. And that's my promise to you if you read and apply these simple principles:

THE 7 PRINCIPLES WILL TRANSFORM YOUR THINKING!

YOU'LL DISCOVER...
...A NEW WAY OF LOOKING AT DEBT
...TOOLS FOR OVERCOMING BARRIERS TO FINANCIAL FREEDOM
...PRACTICAL STEPS FOR BUILDING LONG-TERM WEALTH

Best of all, I can make you these promises *regardless* of your background, income level, or current financial circumstances!

CHANGE YOUR THINKING...AND YOUR DESTINY

As an ex-mortgage lender and financial coach, I've had an opportunity to work with many wealthy people, and I've frequently asked them their secrets to financial success. I'll share more about this later in the book...and some of their answers may surprise you.

But let me mention just one fact that I've found particularly interesting:

**WEALTHY PEOPLE USUALLY PROSPER *REGARDLESS*
OF WHAT HAPPENS IN THE ECONOMY.**

Isn't that rather astonishing? How can these successful people not only *survive* economic tsunamis, but *thrive* in them?

In sharp contrast to my encounters with the wealthy, I meet many people who constantly struggle with their finances. Whether the national economy is up or down, they never seem to get ahead.

Why is there such a wide chasm between the experiences of the wealthy and the poor? Is it merely fate, something preordained by God and impossible to change? *Not at all!*

God wants to bless His people with abundance. But in order to receive that abundance, we must follow His principles—the Golden Rules of finances described in Scripture.

But don't miss this critical fact:

**THE RICH *THINK DIFFERENTLY* ABOUT
MONEY THAN THE POOR DO.**

No wonder this is true, for the Bible says transformation only comes "by the renewing of your mind" (Romans 12:2). To be transformed in our financial circumstances—or any other area of our lives—*we must have our minds renewed.*

Are you ready for your thinking to change? I hope so, because your economic destiny depends on it!

DISCOVERING A FOOLPROOF PLAN

During my search for solid financial solutions that would benefit my family and my clients, I had a simple revelation:

IN ADDITION TO HAVING A DIVINE PURPOSE FOR EACH OF US, GOD ALSO HAS AN *ECONOMIC* PLAN FOR OUR LIVES.

Just as the Lord wants us to be successful in fulfilling our assignment in life, He also expects us to be faithful to His economic plan. He wants us to be good managers over what He's entrusted to our care. Regardless of our profession or income level, we must learn to properly manage the time, talents and resources He has given us during our time on earth.

Contrary to what many people think, I began to realize that our destiny does not happen automatically. Instead, the *outcomes* in our lives are determined by the *choices* we make and how we *manage* what we have.

It also became clear to me that financial success is not a matter of randomly "winning life's lottery," as some people suggest. There are well-defined principles governing economic success. Just like the law of gravity, these principles produce predictable outcomes for anyone applying them, regardless of their background, education or upbringing.

Yet if you're accustomed to reading the financial books at Borders or watching the Wall Street gurus on cable TV programs, you might come up with an entirely different view—that there are NO hard and fast rules for handling money. Everything seems sub-

YOUR
Economic Destiny

jective and debatable, whether the topic is the national debt or your personal debt.

IN CONTRAST WITH THE TRANSITORY AND INCONSISTENT VIEWS OF FINANCIAL PUNDITS...
THESE 7 KEYS ARE MORE THAN JUST ANOTHER SET OF ECONOMIC OPINIONS OR FADS. THEY'RE IRREFUTABLE, TIME-TESTED TRUTHS THAT WORK TO OUR ADVANTAGE IF WE FOLLOW THEM OR TO OUR DETRIMENT IF WE IGNORE THEM.

While I sometimes say I "discovered" the 7 keys, they actually aren't "new" at all. In fact, most of them are taken right out of the pages of Scripture. Rather than merely being "theoretical" truths, they work in the *real world*. They've been life-changing for me and my clients—and they'll be life-changing for you as well.

But let's be honest: Many people who can quote Bible verses or other economic wisdom are still living in a financial wasteland. They can talk a good game, but they struggle to *implement* the truths they know. They keep thinking they "should have known better" than their economic track record has demonstrated, yet somehow a vital component is missing.

If this is *your* situation, don't worry. Help is on the way! In this book...

I'LL DESCRIBE SIMPLE, REVOLUTIONARY TOOLS THAT WILL ENABLE YOU TO *IMPLEMENT* THE 7 PRINCIPLES ON AN ONGOING BASIS.

For many of my clients, these tools have provided the *missing link* for their financial success.

BEWARE OF FOOL'S GOLD

Something alarming is taking place in the financial services industry today. Paid for with billion-dollar advertising budgets, a plethora of agenda-driven, fad-based, "Mc Finance" messages are being shouted from our airwaves and educational institutions. As a result, we've seen unproven, greed-driven, shortsighted financial concepts replace the basic, common-sense principles that formed the successful economic foundation we received from our Founding Fathers, parents and grandparents.

THE 7 PRINCIPLES OF FINANCE HAVE BEEN REPLACED WITH FOOL'S GOLD!

I know what I'm talking about, because for many years I followed plausible-sounding financial plans that led me to fool's gold instead of the 7 *principles* of God's economic plan. And even after I began to discover God's principles of finance, I felt compelled to test them out before sharing them with others.

So I decided I must embark on a personal journey—a kind of due diligence process—to either prove these principles true or show them to be outdated and ineffective. Like any valid scientific experiment, I began by trying to *disprove* these financial laws and then carefully worked backwards to see if there were any missing links in the chain.

As I'll share a little later in the book, I didn't have to search very far for an opportunity to put these principles to the test. Out of nowhere, my wife Carrie and I were faced with "a perfect economic storm."

WHY CARE ABOUT MY STORY?

In the next few chapters, I'll take you on an adventure through the hazardous financial storm my wife and I had to confront in order to discover the tools we were lacking. And even if you aren't particularly interested in what my wife and I went through, I think you'll find that our discoveries are a great benefit in your *own* financial journey.

Honestly, storms can be scary. And like a tsunami that strikes without warning, an economic storm can do great damage.

You or a loved one may already have experienced devastation to marriage, children, health, faith or even sanity—all because of a financial tsunami. And while there's no doubt that the world's economic situation will be extremely perilous in the coming years, you don't have to be unprepared.

Of course, the struggles Carrie and I experienced are not particularly unique these days. Many people have gone through similar economic crises.

But it's one thing to go through storms, and another thing to *learn* from them. And I found it wasn't good enough merely to learn some raw principles for financial success—I also had to consistently *apply* them to my life.

At the risk of spoiling the mystery, let me tell you in advance: *Our story has a happy ending!* Through God's grace, Carrie and I were empowered to overcome the financial disaster many Americans are experiencing today.

If you've had your own financial struggles, you'll be able to relate to our story. And if you're *still* in the middle of your own economic storm, I pray you'll be encouraged by the way God used these 7 principles to bring about a triumphant outcome for Carrie and me.

Through our trials—and the lessons we were able to learn—God has given us a passion to help others escape the bondage of debt, build long-term, purpose-driven wealth, and experience financial freedom at last.

FOLLOW ME ON THIS EXCITING JOURNEY, AS WE DISCOVER THE 7 PRINCIPLES THAT WILL TRANSFORM YOUR OWN ECONOMIC DESTINY...AND THE GENERATIONS TO COME!

AND REMEMBER...

I didn't write this book to give you knowledge for knowledge's sake—I wrote it to GIVE YOU A FINANCIAL TRANSFORMATION!

PART ONE:
MY STORY OF
DESPERATION
TO DESTINY

Chapter 1

READY TO RUN
MY PERSONAL ECONOMIC STORM

"Change can only take place when the desire to change outweighs the desire to stay the same." —Les Brown

"Success is the ability to go from one failure to another with no loss of enthusiasm." —Winston Churchill

A NOTE TO READERS: *This is a difficult and humbling story to tell, but it's the truth. If the truth must be told to help you and others find hope in your own economic storms, then it's well worth it to lay aside my pride and share this ironic story.*

"What's the irony?" you ask. Simply this: After being looked up to for many years by my clients and my peers in the financial services industry, I was nearly destroyed by my own financial mistakes. And it's also ironic that someone who encountered such financial bondage can now hand you powerful keys that will bring you financial liberty. There was hope for me—and now there's hope for you as well. —Jeff

IT WAS A NIGHT I'LL NEVER FORGET. Though I never could have guessed it at the time, this stormy night marked the turning of the tide in my economic destiny.

I restlessly watched from bed as thunder and lightning rolled in across the lake just outside our house. Our bedroom filled with bright flashes of light as bolts of lightning touched down all around our property.

Whenever the lightning flashes dimmed, I took special notice of the 12-foot floor-to-ceiling windows that stretched across the back of our master bedroom wall, giving us a beautiful view of the lake on sunny days—and the storm tonight.

As I viewed the splendor of it all, it occurred to me that we didn't have any curtains on those massive windows.

Where *were* the curtains anyway? Oh yeah, we couldn't afford them.

My wife Carrie and I had recently moved into the home of our dreams after coming to the Carolinas from the West Coast. We were opening up another of our mortgage offices and intending to launch a live radio talk show dealing with financial issues. The projected name of the program was "The Mortgage Answer Man," and we hoped to help our listeners make better financial decisions.

Our vision for the show was born out of witnessing some destructive trends hit the real estate market. So many people had bought into the idea that real estate was the hottest thing since the California gold rush, and we felt that some caution was needed. People with very little financial knowledge were making life-altering decisions based on the ill-considered advice of loan officers, bankers, real estate agents, financial planners, CPAs, brokers, and attorneys.

Sadly, many of these advisors either were financially illiterate themselves, or else their advice was influenced by the prospect of receiving some form of monetary gain from the transaction. This was disturbing to me. Instead of cautioning their clients about the dangers of assuming major long-term debt, these professionals seemed motivated primarily by a desire for personal profit.

Meanwhile, our plans for a one-hour weekly radio program weren't working out as fast as we'd hoped, primarily because of a lack of funding.

"Why the lack of funding?" you ask. "I thought you were a hot-shot financial guru!"

Well, two months after our move to the Carolinas, the entire West Coast real estate market began to crash—and that had been our main source of income! The downturn happened so quickly that our income decreased 75% in just four months.

The little income we had was barely enough to cover the basics of food, gas and electricity. We couldn't even afford to purchase a full-size refrigerator for the new home, so we used a wine chiller that barely held four days worth of food and one carton of milk.

Despite how desperate our situation sounds, we were still lying in a king-size bed layered with Egyptian cotton sheets, in a master bedroom with double-tray lighting and built-in overhead surround sound.

What were we doing in a place like this, when we couldn't even afford to purchase something as basic as curtains and a new refrigerator?

As our bank account and food supply were shrinking, our dream house seemed to grow bigger and bigger, and I was feeling smaller and smaller. Our hopes and dreams were turning into an uncontrollable nightmare of despair and lack.

I lay awake each night, unable to stop the thoughts of what would happen to us if our situation didn't turn around soon. My mind churned with hopelessness and fear, wondering what the next day might bring. I was concerned we might not be able to keep the few things we had left—everything we had worked so hard for.

In fear of facing the evidence of our plight, I stopped opening the mail until a week or so after it arrived. Late notices and collection demands were piling up fast. After 5:00 p.m. most days, the phone in my home office began to ring, and it continued ringing until all hours of the night. No, the callers didn't want my advice on mortgages…they were bill collectors calling about our late payments.

COLD SWEAT

As I lay wide awake in bed that stormy night, feeling totally hopeless and frustrated, a cold sweat began to form on my body. Anxiety filled my mind and tightness gripped my chest, all because I couldn't stop thinking about the worst things that could happen.

Unanswerable questions continually filled my mind. What could I have done differently? How could I get us out of this mess? Were we going to end up losing our home? Where would we go? Would we end up on the street? Would our cars be taken away? Why didn't we have a contingency plan?

And what about our dogs? They're part of our family. What would happen to them if we had to move into a hotel or apartment? Would they end up in someone else's care? If so, would they truly be loved and cared for?

As my mind raced with random thoughts of dread, I felt tormented by the unknown—feelings I hadn't experienced since the passing of my father when I was just 13 years old.

What did I do to deserve this? Where had I gone wrong? Were these consequences from some wrongdoing? Had I failed to ask for forgiveness for something in my past? Or was this simply my destiny, after all?

I found myself questioning both my ability and my worthiness. Perhaps I was incompetent to manage a home, a marriage, or a business. And although I had always considered myself a good person—honest, hardworking, and compassionate toward others—maybe I was wrong...

WHOSE TO BLAME?

Desperate to find relief from all this self-doubt and self-condemnation, I looked for others to blame. Carrie, my wife, lying next to me in bed, had been involved in most of the financial decisions we'd made. She even handled most of the accounting. Hadn't I told her we shouldn't risk buying a home this big, just because we were making good money and thought we could afford it?

18

Blame

What had Carrie been thinking? That our income would inevitably continue to increase? That we simply were *entitled* to a big house and lavish lifestyle? *entitlement*

This has got to be her fault, not mine. Didn't Eve give Adam the apple?

Suddenly I realized I had given into most of Carrie's wishes, all in the name of marital peace. I should have stood up to her more... for her own good. *How could I have been so stupid and naïve?*

For over an hour, my confused and angry thoughts wrestled within me, seeking some kind of resolution and peace. Meanwhile, the person I loved the most was being cast as my archenemy. Instead of seeing her as my better half and best friend, my twisted mind was viewing her as a corrupt business partner who was out to get me.

I knew I had to snap out of this and get some sleep. None of my introspection or blame-shifting made me feel any better or provided any solutions to the mess we were in.

Tossing the covers back, I rolled over again and planted my face deep into the pillow. I hoped I would soon cool down and be able to quiet the tormenting thoughts that plagued my mind...but nothing seemed to help my downward spiral into despair.

Meanwhile, Carrie was sound asleep, totally unaware of the war raging inside the man lying next to her. *How could she sleep so soundly, when I was terrified and felt like running away?*

But where could I run to? I didn't have enough money to get very far. And 35-year-old men don't run away from home, do they?

19

Chapter 2

HEARING VOICES

SUDDENLY MY DESPAIRING THOUGHTS were overcome by a voice and tone much different from my own.

> *"Jeff, get out of bed and go upstairs. There is*
> *something in the attic I want you to see."*

"What?" I answered.

I turned over to see if Carrie had woken up or was talking in her sleep. But she was still sleeping.

I must really be going mad, I thought. No one else was in the room except for us and the dogs, and I had never heard the dogs mutter anything more than a few grunts when they we're begging for some food off my plate.

I concluded that the voice must be coming from my own state of dementia. But just in case there was something more to it, I decided I'd better check to see if there really *was* something significant in the attic.

I rolled out of bed as quietly as possible, careful not to wake Carrie. That was the *last* thing I wanted to explain: *"Honey, I'm being called upstairs to the attic by a strange voice. Don't worry, I'll be back in a minute!"*

I planted my feet on the floor and quietly made my way out of the bedroom and up the wooden staircase into the attic. Opening the small attic door, I saw nothing out of place.

If the "voice" was correct, what was I supposed to find up here?

I noticed a pile of cardboard boxes filled with stuff I had planned to unpack someday. Could there be something in the boxes that would solve our financial problems? Was there a check I failed to cash...a forgotten money jar...a winning lottery ticket...a valuable heirloom or piece of jewelry?

This is crazy! I shook my head in disappointment at my deteriorating mental state. But as I turned to close the door and leave, I noticed a white cardboard box filled with books. Figuring I might as well try to read myself to sleep, I reached into the box and randomly dug around until I felt a paperback run across my hand, almost giving me a paper cut.

I determined that this must be a new book, since it felt sturdy and unwrinkled. I grabbed it, turned off the attic light, and slowly made my way back down the stairs and into the living room. The couch seemed the best place for me to do a little reading without disturbing Carrie.

As I stretched out on the couch and reached over to see what book I had plucked from the box, I was surprised that I had never seen it before. I'm an avid reader and usually know all the books in my library.

In light of our current struggles, the book's title read like a sick joke:

GOD'S PLANS FOR YOUR FINANCES

Where did we get this book? I couldn't imagine.

The book's bold title seemed to mock me, yet somehow I was drawn to open it. What could I lose? If it was full of boring platitudes, it might help me go to sleep. If it had an uplifting message, it might help to drive away my discouragement and hopelessness.

But what a strange name for a book. If God had any kind of a plan for my finances, I surely would like to know about it. My *own* plans definitely weren't getting me anywhere.

Yet I was skeptical that this book would have any real answers for my situation. It probably was some get-rich-quick formula...or maybe a treatise on the "Prosperity Gospel."

Instead of starting at the beginning of the book or flipping to the ending, I opened it right smack in the middle. I usually can tell within minutes if a book is worth my time.

My eyes went directly to some bold words in the middle of the page:

RIGHT IN THE HEAD BUT WRONG IN THE HEART

Hmmm...sounded like an interesting concept.

The rest of the paragraph was a short story about a businessman who was trying to run his business on Biblical principles, and it went something like this: While listening to his preacher's message about "giving" the prior Sunday, the businessman was really inspired by the statement, "You can't out give God!"

The man went back to his business and emptied out his entire cash drawer and reserve account to put it in the offering plate the following Sunday. Unfortunately, even though his intentions were good, this decision put his business in jeopardy and caused him major problems in paying his bills for a while.

"It's useless to attempt to run a business on Biblical principles," he concluded. "Business is business, and the Bible is only a bunch of instructions on how to get to heaven."

I was about to applaud this businessman's conclusion, when the author continued: "Wait a minute...not so fast! You can't just toss out running your business on Biblical principles. This man *misapplied* what the Bible says!"

By now I was intrigued. This man had clearly done his best to take action on the preacher's message, but the results were disastrous. Where had he gone wrong?

The author explained that you can't just pick out one principle to base your actions upon. Instead, God's principles must be applied in *combination* with each other—so you can't expect to benefit from one principle if you're breaking another one.

While it seemed noble for the businessman to "give the business's money to God," this ignored some other important factors: Was all the money actually his to give? Wasn't some of the money already committed to such things as bills, employee salaries, and taxes?

The author pointed out that if the money was already committed to prior obligations, then it didn't belong to him in the first place. *You can't give away what is not yours to give! That is called stealing.* Without realizing it, the man had broken one principle in hopes of profiting from another.

In trying to implement the preacher's message, the businessman failed to see the full picture. He didn't realize that God will never tell you to do something in violation of a principle He's already given you. In this case, the man had unwittingly violated the principles of honesty and integrity. The money that belonged to the business was not money he could legitimately take—it was only his to *manage*.

The author concluded:

"IGNORANCE IS NOT A GOOD EXCUSE. YOU MUST UNDERSTAND THAT GOD WANTS OUR HEARTS AND OUR ACTIONS TO LINE UP WITH ALL THE PRINCIPLES HE'S GIVEN US IN HIS WORD."

Wow, this is good stuff! I wondered what principles *I'd* been breaking because of ignorance.

However, it was very hard for me to accept the possibility that my financial calamities were the result of broken Biblical principles. Rationalizations flooded my mind:

Hey, I'm probably just the victim of a really bad economy. My business is mortgage lending, and the whole industry is in the toilet right now.

Breaking Biblical principles? Hey, I've taken care of my clients with integrity, and I've even sacrificed to help out people who were in financial distress.

No, this personal financial meltdown couldn't possibly be my fault!

There was no way I could accept the blame for this. The fault *had* to lie elsewhere.

And what about tithing? I've faithfully tithed 10% right off the top of my income—shouldn't that count for something? Isn't God obligated to bless the other 90% of my income and let me spend it however I like?

Suddenly I realized that I had fallen into the same trap as the businessman in the story, not realizing I was just the *manager* of my income, not the *owner*. I had thought that if I tithed, prayed, and thanked God for my blessings, then He would *automatically* take care of all my needs.

Yet something was missing in this equation. Were there additional principles I was unintentionally neglecting?

My tired mind was still racing…reeling…rationalizing. *Many other good people were in financial trouble,* I reasoned in my defense. *Had they all broken Biblical financial principles too?*

Finally I decided to try again to get some sleep before my brain blew a circuit. I drifted off in a restless, dream-filled slumber, praying I soon would receive some loan approvals to put my clients at ease and put some money in our empty bank account.

Chapter 3
A TROUBLED CONSCIENCE

THE NEXT DAY BEGAN like just another normal day at the office: working through the ever-tightening lending regulations and trying to fit my clients' loans into the new industry guidelines. This was becoming an increasingly frustrating process, akin to forcing a square peg into a round hole—a hole that was getting smaller by the minute.

But I had been praying for more business, and sure enough, later in the day I *did* receive a call from a client. He was a friend from California I had helped with several real estate transactions over the years, and the conversation went something like this...

"Hi Charlie. What can I help you with?" My mind raced...*Was this an answer to my prayer the previous night? Did Charlie need a refinance or new loan I could help him with?* God surely knew I needed some income to keep the business going.

"Hello, Jeff, my favorite loan officer," Charlie began. "Yes, I'm in need of some help. I know you're an honest man and blessed with God's favor, so I think you can solve my problem."

"OK, Charlie, what's up?" I asked in a confident tone of voice, eager to solve any dilemma he could throw my way.

"Well, Jeff, I have some good news and some bad news. The good news is that the value of homes in our neighborhood are still strong despite all the other foreclosures happening in the valley below us. The bad news is that I've lost my job."

"I'm sorry to hear that, Charlie."

"But Jeff, I think I have a plan that will work. My dad is also on the title to my home, and even though he hasn't lived here for a number of years, he and my mom are moving back so I can get this loan done. Since they were on the original loan, you might be able to use their income and credit to qualify for the new one."

I was already getting uncomfortable with this conversation, but Charlie continued: "In order to keep our home, we need a much lower payment. I got a flyer in the mail last week, and it says we can get a 1% interest rate. That sounds awesome! The problem is, I called the bank offering that deal, and they're charging way too much for their fees. I know you're the expert, Jeff, and with all the business I've brought you over the years, I'm sure you'll be gracious to us."

Charlie sure was laying the compliments on thick. "Thank you for thinking of me, Charlie. I always appreciate your business. But are you familiar with the risks of that kind of adjustable rate loan? If the market doesn't come back, you could lose your home or the payment could *double* at the end of the fixed-rate period!"

"Jeff, I'm not really concerned about that right now," Charlie insisted. "I'm just concerned about keeping a roof over my head. God has given us this house, and I believe that if we have a lower monthly payment for a while, He will take care of the rest. You don't think God wants my family out on the street, do you?!"

"Well, no...not at all, Charlie. I just want to make sure you really want this type of loan and understand what it will mean."

"Yes, Jeff, and I want to do the loan with *you*...as long as you don't have to charge us any more than one point on the deal. OK?"

Suddenly the reality of that hit me. On a home loan of that size, one point would mean a $6,000 commission for me! *Wow, this might be an answer to our prayers!*

"Well, Charlie, I totally understand, and I think I can get that loan done for you. I know exactly what bank to take it to, and I'll see if I can lock that rate in for you guys today."

"Thanks, Jeff," Charlie said appreciatively as the call concluded. "You're the man!"

UNEASY FEELINGS

Despite this apparent windfall in answer to my prayers, I was still feeling uneasy about Charlie's objective. Washington Mutual was the only lender still doing that kind of a loan, and somehow they still seemed to be going strong despite the overall market downturn.

I got on the phone right away to see if Washington Mutual still had that loan program available, and to my surprise, they did. However, my account representative at Washington Mutual said I had better act fast, since that program would expire at 6:00 p.m. Eastern Standard Time that day. If my customer really wanted that program, it had to be locked in before then.

I found out later that I had just locked in one of the last option-ARM loans Washington Mutual would ever do.

Casting my concerns aside, I was thrilled to finally have some income on the horizon. This really made my day!

After an early dinner with my lovely bride—and the accompanying dogs that warmed our feet under the dinner table—I decided to retire to the bedroom a little earlier than normal. On the way, I stopped at the coffee table and picked up the book I had found in the attic the night before.

Still exhausted from the hours of wrestling with fear and hopelessness the night before, I stretched out on the bed, fluffed my pillow just right, and started reading the book from the very beginning.

Carrie also came to bed early to read. Peering over her Bible, she asked me what book I was reading.

"Just something I started last night," I said vaguely.

"Last night? Did you get out of bed after the storm passed?"

"Yes, I couldn't fall asleep, so I went out to the couch to read for a while."

Not wanting to tell her that the book and I were magically paired by a voice that called me upstairs to the attic, I added, "I just grabbed a book at random to rest my mind. Good night, Carrie. I love you."

"I love you too, Jeffrey." Carrie put her Bible down and immediately fell fast asleep, as usual. I have no idea how she does that. It's as if she doesn't have a care in the world.

I'm almost sure Carrie's blood type is *"Be Positive"*...but my own cares weren't so easy to dispel.

Chapter 4
TRANSFORMING A DESTINY

WITH CARRIE FAST ASLEEP, it was time for me to delve into the mystery hidden within the pages of this book. After years in the financial services industry, I couldn't imagine that this book would contain a message I had somehow overlooked...a message that would calm my hopelessness and transform my future.

But after making my way past the introduction and first chapter, I began to realize there was indeed something very special about this book's message. It probably wasn't "new." I must have read something similar before. Yet somehow it had never really sunk in. *How could I have missed it all these years?*

The message was basically very simple...

JUST AS GOD CREATED A PHYSICAL UNIVERSE THAT RUNS ON SPECIFIC LAWS, HE ALSO CREATED AN ECONOMIC SYSTEM BASED ON ASCERTAINABLE LAWS AND PRINCIPLES.

Wow, that made sense! Why wouldn't the One who created the rules governing this complex universe *also* have an economic system based on specific principles that govern our financial success?

I already understood that God has a master plan for people's eternal salvation, so why would it seem strange that He *also* has a plan for how we're supposed to manage our financial resources? How ironic that, despite being a Christian with years of experience in the financial services industry, I had never thought much about God's plan for our financial decisions.

ECONOMIC ILLITERACY?

This book was raising lots of good questions.

For years I had the simplistic notion that if people simply got some education, acquired job skills, and worked hard, they would end up doing just fine. On the other hand, I figured that those who are lazy and unmotivated would end up being poor.

And of course, I already knew there were spiritual principles like "Give and it shall be given to you" (Luke 6:38). But I didn't realize there are many *other* economic laws—laws that are just as certain as the law of gravity.

Since we spend most of our lives getting an education and then working for money, how come most people's education doesn't include *financial* literacy as well as learning our ABCs and 123s? Why are there required courses about the laws of physics or chemistry, but an absence of instruction about the laws of financial success?

The more I pondered these questions, the angrier I became:

WHY WASN'T I TAUGHT THESE FINANCIAL LAWS IN SCHOOL... OR EVEN IN SUNDAY SCHOOL? WHY DIDN'T I EVER HAVE A CLASS ABOUT THE PRINCIPLES GOVERNING FINANCIAL INCREASE AND ABUNDANCE?

As wonderful as it is to learn about math, science, the arts or literature, how sad that most people's education has not included a solid economic foundation. Even college level courses in economics and business seldom teach the principles of personal money management.

CLIENT BEWARE

By now it was 2:00 a.m., and I was having a hard time putting this book down. In addition to discovering great principles for transforming my personal finances, I couldn't help but think about all my clients over the years. I had been in a position to help them make major financial decisions—choices that would alter their lives for many years to come. *Did they know about these principles?*

As I turned a page and read another principle, my conversation with Charlie suddenly flooded back to my mind. There it was: *My client Charlie was going to break a vital financial principle, and I was about to break another one by helping him obtain his loan.*

How could breaking these principles end well? Someone might jump off the Empire State Building, thinking he could break the law of gravity and float up to the clouds. But the law of gravity will prove itself true, despite their sincere misconception. In the same way, those who break the principles governing financial success will inevitably suffer the consequences...whether they understood the principles or not.

I began to ponder how all of this applied to my current financial situation. My conscious was tormented by the lessons I was receiving from this book. I already was in a dire situation...would things get even *worse* for me if I proceeded with Charlie's loan?

"OH LORD," I PLEADED, "WHY AM I BEING EXPOSED TO THESE PRINCIPLES NOW? I'M ALREADY IN A MAJOR FINANCIAL MESS, AND I REALLY NEED THE COMMISSION FROM CHARLIE'S REFINANCE LOAN. AND WON'T IT HELP HIS FAMILY SAVE THEIR HOME IF THEY CAN GET A LOWER MONTHLY PAYMENT?"

What a terrible dilemma. Although I was grateful to receive these amazing new insights about God's financial plan, from all appearances, it would make my *immediate* situation even worse.

WHAT TO DO ABOUT CHARLIE

I decided to delay believing and implementing the author's message until I'd taken time to look up the principles in the Bible. *Surely* God would want me to help Charlie, and I wanted to use my education and training to get it done quickly.

With the volatility in the mortgage industry, I knew that even one day's delay could end his chances of refinancing. How would I feel if I knew I could have helped his family but failed to act fast enough—all because of some book I'd found in the attic?! How self-righteous and unprofessional that would be!

In my heart of hearts, I wanted to learn and obey the truth—but perhaps not quite yet. So my rationalizations continued...

It would be idiotic for me to just take this author's word for everything! Maybe he's just taking Scripture verses out of context and twisting them to sell his books. I need to look this stuff up for myself.

And how do I know the ancient wisdom of the Bible can provide sound financial advice for complex 21st-century problems? It's a great book and all, but lots of things have changed in the past 2,000 years, right?

The more I rationalized, the more turmoil filled my heart. But the more I read this book, the more hopeful I became that God truly *could* transform my financial destiny.

Chapter 5 ————————————

THIRSTY FOR KNOWLEDGE

D ESPITE THE LATE HOUR, I continued to thumb through the rest of the book. Some of the advice was much the same as all the other financial books: create a budget, live below your means, don't buy new cars, refinance your home if the offered interest rate is 2 percent lower, get a 15-year mortgage, buy term life insurance and invest the difference in your 401(k), etc., etc.

This part of the book was stuff I had all heard before. What a disappointment! Instead of ground-breaking, life-changing keys to transform people's finances, it was the "same old, same old."

Over the years, I had already concluded that something was missing from most of the traditional "debt diet" books. Although their advice sounds good in theory and often provides a certain amount of short-term relief, I found that very few people achieve lasting transformation. Much like yo-yo food diets leave people overweight, these debts diets usually leave people right back where they started—still in debt.

Think about it: Like a broken record, various versions of the debt diet have now been proclaimed by books, media and seminars for more than 25 years now. If these programs truly brought permanent transformation to people in the real world, wouldn't a lot more people be out of bondage to debt by now?

In my experience, it takes the discipline of an army sergeant to make the kinds of sacrifices required by traditional debt diets. How long can people live on beans and rice? What if they buy clunkers instead of new cars—only to be overwhelmed by constant repair bills?

Somehow there's got to be some balance. On the one hand, some fiscal discipline and restraint is certainly needed in most of our lives (not to mention in our national government). But on the other hand, we all need to "live a little," lest we turn into a bunch of disgruntled sourpusses. And didn't Jesus promise to give us an abundant life instead of one of constant deprivation? (John 10:10)

Of course, many of the debt diet books include some sound Biblical truths—principles that will work for anyone IF they are set in the proper context. But people often get sidetracked by the practical applications these authors try to make.

Frankly, some of the lopsided advice comes from *male* authors who need to have a little more understanding and compassion toward women. Their advice would never fly in my house!

For example, it's one thing if a *man* wants to drive a car that's falling apart, has questionable brakes, and requires a fresh quart of oil every week. But don't expect me to put *my* bride or other loved ones in a vehicle like that! I'm not willing to risk an accident or have Carrie stranded alongside a highway just to save a few bucks each month.

CHARLIE ON MY MIND

By now it was 3:00 a.m. I was still pondering the book...and still wondering what the Bible would instruct me to do about Charlie's situation. I felt a serious responsibility in this, almost as if Charlie's entire financial destiny was dangling from my fingertips.

GIVE ME WISDOM IN THIS, LORD. IF THE BIBLE TRULY HAS ANSWERS FOR CHARLIE'S SITUATION, PLEASE SHOW ME...

No sooner had I whispered this prayer, than I drifted off for some brief and much-needed sleep. Although my mental gymnastics hadn't fully ended, I had found a measure of peace in surrendering the whole matter to God.

The next day was a productive one, despite my lack of sleep. After gathering everything I needed to submit Charlie's loan to Washington Mutual, I decided to head to bed early. But as I made my way to the bedroom, I started thinking about what I had read the night before.

Oh yeah, I was going to look in my Bible and see what it says about my efforts to help Charlie.

Before even opening my Bible, I started thinking of some things I had read years before from Larry Burkett, pioneer of the "You can live debt-free" movement in America. He warned people to avoid "surety," which he defined as "making a debt or commitment without having a sure way to repay the debt."

Burkett went on to describe surety as taking responsibility for, or making a commitment of time and money to, something where the amount owed is more than the object is worth. Based on Burkett's definition, credit cards must be the worst form of breaking the surety principle.

But what about Charlie? Wasn't he about to place himself and his parents in a surety position? Did his parents understand the surety principle and the consequences they could face for breaking it?

And what about me? What consequences would I reap if I put them into a surety position?

LOSING MORE SLEEP

I had hoped this would be a peaceful and sleep-filled night, but here I was again, wrestling with what the Bible teaches about money, surety and debt. I was beginning to feel really uncomfortable again as I reached for my Bible to see if it supported Burkett's interpretation of the surety principle.

I thumbed through numerous pages of Scripture before finally arriving at these verses in the book of Proverbs:

Do not be one who shakes hands in pledge or puts up security for debts; if you lack the means to pay, your very bed will be snatched from under you. (Proverbs 22:26-27 NIV)

The New Living Translation renders this same passage:

Don't agree to guarantee another person's debt or put up security for someone else. If you can't pay it, even your bed will be snatched from under you.

And other verses confirm this same warning:

He who puts up security for another will surely suffer, but whoever refuses to strike hands in pledge is safe (Proverbs 11:15 NIV).

An even more detailed verse on the same subject:

My son, if you become surety for your friend, If you have shaken hands in pledge for a stranger,

You are snared by the words of your mouth; You are taken by the words of your mouth.

So do this, my son, and deliver yourself; For you have come into the hand of your friend: Go and humble yourself; Plead with your friend.

Give no sleep to your eyes, Nor slumber to your eyelids.

Deliver yourself like a gazelle from the hand of the hunter, And like a bird from the hand of the fowler (Proverbs 6:1-5).

Wow, how could Scripture be any clearer? A wave of deep conviction swept over me as I thought of the many times I had aided people in breaking this financial principle and most of the banks were encouraging this! I couldn't just wash my hands of responsibility—or consequences.

But now I was faced with a critical decision. If I chose to ignore what I had just learned, I would be breaking *another* principle...the principle of honesty and integrity. Difficult as it was, I had to make Charlie aware that he was about to make a big mistake. If we went through with that specific kind of loan and, more importantly, used *his parent's credit* for collateral, we would be breaking the surety principle.

I couldn't afford to lose anymore sleep, but I knew that's what would happen if I continued to wrestle against what I was learning. I had no alternative but to warn Charlie about the negative consequences he and his parents would face if they proceeded with the loan.

DECISION TIME

The next day I woke up with Charlie and his parents still on my mind. I had to tell Charlie what I was learning about the surety principle.

But how will Charlie react if I warn him about this? He will probably tell me I'm crazy and then go to someone else to handle the loan. If that's the case, shouldn't I just do the loan myself? Ultimately, it's his decision, isn't it?

All my rationalizations had returned. The bottom line was that we really *needed* the big commission Charlie's loan would bring. It would mean a roof over our heads for at least another month or so. And how could I ever explain to Carrie why I passed up thousands of dollars in commissions, just to stand on a principle I had just discovered?

But I knew I had entered the mortgage business to help people win financially, not to sink them deeper into bondage. At all costs, I had to maintain my integrity and quit flirting with financial compromise. By this time I was feeling weak and a little sick. The spiritual and ethical battle was taking its toll.

It was now 4:00 a.m., and I had made my decision! I would not do Charlie's loan, regardless of the short-term financial consequences to my family or his. Even though Carrie and I desperately needed the money, it wasn't worth compromising my values.

AN UNCOMFORTABLE PHONE CALL

I arrived early to the office the next morning. As I sat down at my desk and peered out the window, I noticed something hovering in the tree. It was a blue jay picking berries from a long, skinny branch. Suddenly, I began to recall these words spoken by Jesus:

Look at the birds of the air, for they neither sow nor reap nor gather into barns; yet your heavenly Father feeds them. Are you not of more value than they? (Matthew 6:26)

Just as God was taking care of that blue jay, surely He would take care of Carrie and me as well. I could stay strong, do the right thing, and leave the consequences to Him and He would meet our needs!

Finally the bird finished his breakfast and flew away, leaving me to read my e-mails, check out the day's best interest rates…and focus on the mountain of paperwork to be faxed into Washington Mutual on Charlie's behalf.

I had barely begun, when the phone rang. A little surprised that the phone had rung so early, I answered: "Hello, and thank you for calling. How may I help you?"

"Hello, Jeff. This is Charlie. Did you get the information I faxed you on my parents' retirement income?"

"Yes, Charlie, I did. I'm holding the loan package in my hand right now."

"Well, what are you waiting for, Jeff? Let's get this loan on the road."

"Ahh, well…Charlie, I need to talk to you about something really important." I was beginning to feel squeamish about this again. I realized I was sounding more like a high school guidance counselor than a mortgage broker, yet I continued: "You believe in God, don't you, Charlie?"

"Yes," he replied in a low, overbearing tone of voice, "but what's that have to do with my loan, Jeff?"

"Well, do you believe that the Bible is a good source for finding truth and direction in life?"

"Yes, of course, Jeff. I live my life by the Word, and I even teach the New Members class at my church every Sunday. But I still don't understand what any of that has to do with my mortgage application."

"Charlie, have you ever heard the word 'surety' before?"

"I 'surety' think I have, Jeff. Ha ha ha."

"I'm serious, Charlie. The Bible warns us against entering into surety—assuming responsibility for another person's debt. It's a principle that carries adverse consequences when we violate it."

"Jeff, I'm not sure I understand what you're driving at."

"Here's what I mean, Charlie. If I do this loan for you, it will be putting you and your parents in a position of surety. Although I would really like to do this loan for you, to do so would be going against my better judgment. This has been a difficult decision for me, though—because you need a loan and I need a paycheck. But I just don't feel right about it."

"Have you lost your mind, Jeff?"

"No, Charlie. Actually, I'm beginning to *regain* my mind. I'm just seeing that many people are asking me to help them now that times are tough, but the mortgage solutions aren't really going to help them in the long run. Many of the current options are just financial Band-Aids—short-term solutions to buy them a little more time until all the negative consequences hit."

"Well, I see what you're saying, Jeff. But how does that apply to the loan application we're working on now?"

"Charlie, you have to look ahead instead of just at the short-term. What is going to happen when the introductory minimum payment is gone and your interest rate adjusts? The new payment could be sky high. How are you going to afford it then?"

"I hadn't really thought of that."

"I'm also concerned about what could happen to your parents if the economy gets even worse and you can't make the payments.

They could lose tens of thousands of dollars from their retirement nest egg. That could be catastrophic for them."

"I really thought this could be the perfect solution for me, Jeff."

"Charlie, I know I might sound like a prophet of doom and gloom, but a surety loan like this is no real solution. You could be paying for it the rest of your life, and if something happens to you, your parents won't be able to handle it all by themselves. I don't yet know what the best solution is, but I'm sure if we spend some time asking God for guidance, He will show us what to do."

I held my breath, not sure how Charlie would respond. I'm certain he didn't expect to get a sermon on surety from his loan officer. I thought he might hang up on me, but he didn't.

"Jeff, you probably have something here, and I think you should follow it through on it. If your religious beliefs are getting in the way of helping your customers, perhaps you should rethink your calling in life...this loan business might not be the best place for you. I appreciate your sincere words, but I've got to run now. I've enjoyed doing business with you in the past, because you've always been straight with me. But I have to do what I have to do for my family, and that's just the way I'm going to approach this situation. Have a good day, Jeff."

GOING CRAZY?

I felt awful as I got off the phone with Charlie...

What's wrong with me? In mere minutes, I turned away at least a month's worth of income. I'm not just losing my business, I'm losing my mind!

What will Carrie say when I tell her I turned down helping Charlie get a refinance loan...and now we have nothing?! I'm almost broke, and here I am turning away business in the name of following Biblical financial principles. Maybe I should just call Charlie back and tell him I was all wrong in my comments. But then he would REALLY think I'm flipping my lid!

What could I do but turn to God and ask Him what was happening to me? If He didn't want me in this business anymore, then fine. I just wanted to help people and make a difference in their lives. I wanted to be in a position to serve people and bring them solutions that are truly good for them. How could I stay in a business that kept putting me in a position of choosing between a paycheck and doing what's right?

Even after crying out to God in this short conversation, I still didn't feel any better. In fact, I was beginning to feel lost and hopeless again, without any answers about what direction I should be going.

In desperation, I fell to my knees. My blood pressure rose and hot tears ran down my face as I shouted out God...

"Please give me something to do, something that really helps people! Loans aren't really helping people—they're just causing them to lie, cheat and steal. I can't handle this anymore, Lord. Please show me something different to do. If this is not my destiny, then please open my eyes, give me some direction on what You're proposing for me to do!"

Chapter 6
READY TO GET STARTED

I'M CONVINCED GOD ANSWERS PRAYERS.

Just a day after I cried out to Him to show me ways I could truly help people, He began to unveil exciting new directions for my life. The principles He showed me—which I call the Golden Rules of finances—have already transformed my own economic destiny. Now for the next stage in the process: helping thousands of others break their bondage to debt and discover lasting financial freedom.

But change is seldom easy. Difficult decisions must be made. Patience is required as we await a favorable harvest from the new seeds we've sown.

As God began to reveal His Golden Rules of finances to me, I made a commitment to take them seriously—to change course despite any negative consequences I might temporarily face. I knew I had to trust God and begin taking more personal responsibility for my financial decisions.

I also was deeply aware that God was calling me to impact many other families with the insights He had shown me. That would be impossible without an economic transformation in my own home first.

And there was no time to lose on this—I had to start implementing the principles *immediately* if I expected things to ever change.

Although I was ready to take the first steps in my journey through a financial transformation, I knew I still had a lot to learn. How could I figure out which principles really work, and which ones sound plausible, only to give disappointing results?

SEARCHING FOR A MENTOR

The Bible warns that people are destroyed because of a "lack of knowledge" (Hosea 4:6). I've always enjoyed books, and knowledge has always been very important to me. However, I had already read many books on personal finances, and often their advice was at odds with each other or at odds with the Scriptures. Who could I believe?

It soon became clear that I needed a financial mentor if I was going to make permanent changes in my personal economy. I wanted someone who was in solid shape in their own finances and able to teach me clear and simple ways to implement God's time-tested financial principles.

I knew it was important to find a mentor who "walked their talk." It's relatively easy to write books or present seminars, but what about the testimony of the author's life? Just like new computer software must be "beta tested," I wanted to "test" the mentor's life and his proposed financial principles. What tools did he offer for helping people accomplish their financial goals? And did these tools actually work in the real-world crucible of life?

To my surprise, I discovered that a solid financial mentor isn't always easy to find. After meeting with countless authors and financial gurus in search of help, I was shocked to learn that many of them were in dismal financial shape themselves. How sad that many of them produced great books or seminars but failed to follow their own principles!

Some of the financial mentors weren't in bad financial shape, but I came to discover that their wealth wasn't truly built on sound economic principles. They simply made money by playing the role of a front man or woman for the financial industry, spreading the often-misleading mantras: "buy term life insurance and invest the difference...diversify in Wall Street growth stocks...max-out your 401(k)...refinance your mortgage to a lower rate and shorten your term...cut up your credit cards and pay cash for everything...and so on.

In being true to myself, I had to stop and ponder. If what they are teaching is true, then why isn't everyone just as wealthy as they are, and why aren't these self-professed gurus also wealth coaches to the wealthiest individuals of our world?

The questions persisted: *Who is real...what is solid...and what principles really work?* These were difficult questions to answer! The book market and financial services industry seemed filled with imposters, and advocates of shallow, ineffective solutions. Frustrated with the lack of integrity and inadequate solutions I found, I nearly gave up on my new assignment.

But I refused to accept defeat. There *had* to be answers. I just needed to pray for more divine guidance!

Gradually God answered my prayers and brought me the mentors and the principles I needed to cause a radical transformation in my finances, my career, and the lives of my clients across the country.

**JOIN ME NOW AS I SHARE 7 TIME-TESTED PRINCIPLES
AND TOOLS THAT WILL TRANSFORM YOUR
ECONOMIC DESTINY AS THEY'VE TRANSFORMED MINE.
GET READY FOR THE JOURNEY OF A LIFETIME!**

PART TWO:

7 KEYS THAT WILL TRANSFORM

YOUR ECONOMIC
DESTINY

Chapter 7
UNDERSTANDING YOUR ECONOMIC DESTINY

"If we abide by the principles taught in the Bible, our country will go on prospering...but if we and our prosperity neglect its instructions and authority, no man can tell how sudden a catastrophe may overwhelm us and bury all our glory in profound obscurity."

—Daniel Webster

ONE OF THE PIVOTAL STORIES IN SCRIPTURE describes the journey of the Israelites from bondage in Egypt to freedom in the Promised Land. God has a similar journey for you—bringing you to a place of amazing blessings and abundance.

As we begin this journey, we will need to examine the half-truths and misinformation that have shaped our thinking and choices up to this point. From the outset, we must understand that our minds must be renewed with truth. Until we take this step and are willing to be honest with ourselves, we will never fully realize the depth of our deception.

When you begin to see the incredible financial inheritance God has planned for you, you'll be shocked by how much your thinking has been shaped by messages that run *contrary* to reaching the financial freedom and prosperity you desire to achieve. When you shine the light of truth onto what you've been programmed to believe, you will recognize that many of your financial decisions have undermined the abundance God wants you to have.

God has a plan for you, a purpose and a destiny for your life—and this includes your financial life. His plan started even before you were born, and continues today:

> **Before I formed you in the womb I knew you, before you were born I set you apart (Jeremiah 1:5 NIV).**

> **"I know the plans I have for you," declares the LORD, "plans to prosper you and not to harm you, plans to give you hope and a future" (Jeremiah 29:11).**

God's plan is that we make a difference in the lives of others. If our finances are out of control, we won't have the money—or the time—to meet other people's needs. When we are too busy trying to deal with our *own* cares and problems, we are not able or available to help with the needs of others.

When we lose sight of our economic birthright, we're likely to give up on our dreams. When our time and resources are committed to and controlled by others, this causes the creation of self-imposed barriers that prevent us from reaching our full economic potential.

The average American family is only a few paychecks away from financial disaster. A recent article in a top financial planning magazine stated that 70% of American families are overloaded with debt and living from paycheck to paycheck. Meanwhile, 77% of families have no savings, and 55% are sometimes or always worried about money.

Statistics like these certainly don't seem to mirror divine providence. America was founded for a divine purpose, where freedom, honor, duty, and independence were to remain. Bondage, servitude, and hopelessness were meant to be a thing of the past.

People will spend a great portion of their lives enslaved to mortgage payments and credit card debt. The most productive part of their lives is spent working for the bank to pay down debt on items that have long since lost their value. As a result, their energies are focused on their survival, they have little time or resources left over to impact the lives of others. Even with a good job and what most would consider a good income, they are trapped in a poverty cycle that offers little hope of fulfilling their purpose in life or their financial dreams.

"Too many people spend money they haven't earned to buy things they don't want to impress people they don't like." —Will Rogers

When you read Will Rogers' statement, you might protest, "That's not me! I'm secure in who I am and don't spend money to impress others. I'm just trying to get by and provide good things for my family to enjoy."

While it's a noble objective to provide "good things" for your family, the problem often is in *how* we obtain the funds for those purchases. If we spend our lives using other people's money in the form of credit, we'll inevitably end up in financial bondage. By incurring debt, we voluntarily transfer our freedom to someone else. Unless this process is reversed, it will set the economic tone for the rest of our lives.

God says if we follow His precepts, He will make us "the head, not the tail" (Deuteronomy 28:13). The financial institution that extends us credit becomes "the head," and we become "the tail." Someone else controls our time and resources. Our bondage is caused by a failure to understand and follow basic economic principles.

Whether we realize it or not, many of our financial choices are shaped by the constant drumbeat of alluring messages we hear from financial institutions. Most of us can repeat these messages verbatim, because they've been driven deep into our minds, without our even realizing it.

- "Life takes VISA." —VISA
- "Don't leave home without it." —American Express
- "Chase what matters." —JP Morgan Chase
- "Are you a member?" —American express Gold

- "What's in your wallet?" —Capital One
- "It's everywhere you want to be." —VISA
- "There's always something more to discover." —Discover
- "There are some things money can't buy...for everything else there's Master Card." —Master Card

You can see by the messages above we've been programmed to think there's no way to be successful without debt and credit. But think about it... You definitely don't want some credit card to be your "Master." And you only want to "Chase" what REALLY matters, not what the banks tell you should matter. And I'm sure you can "Discover" a lot more in this life if you're not weighted down with debt!

These relentless ad campaigns can create mental strongholds even for those who have a sincere desire to get their financial circumstances under control. So if we want to be free from financial bondage and fulfill God's purpose for our lives, we must change our thinking!

SHAKESPEARE WAS RIGHT: WE'RE ALL "MERELY PLAYERS"

Instead of being unique to you, financial mistakes are being repeated in households, communities, states and nations throughout the world. As this book is being written, the unsustainable debt in Greece is beginning to send economic shock waves to the ends of the earth. And what about U.S. states like California, that already owe *billions* of dollars they are struggling to repay?

Whether we understand what is happening or not, we are already witnessing the consequences of our individual and national actions. One study found that 80% of the prayer requests in an average church are for health or financial needs—and many of the health issues people experience are related to stress over their financial circumstances. What a contrast to God's stated desire for His people: "Beloved, I pray that you may **prosper** in all things and be in **health**, just as your soul prospers" (3 John 2). Look at these sad statistics found in hundreds of publications about the financial conditions of most American families:

- Less than 3% of American families have 3 to 6 months of savings for emergencies.
- 77% of families have no savings at all.
- 98% of households are burdened with mortgages and credit card debt.
- 70% are living from paycheck to paycheck.
- 40% of families spend more than they earn.
- In 2008 more people filed for bankruptcy than finished college.
- 50% of marriages end in divorce—where money problems are the issue.
- 45% –50% of take-home pay goes to paying debt (principal and interest payments).
- 7 out of 10 individuals will have to depend on the government to cover a portion of their living expenses after retirement.

In addition to distracting us from our life's purpose, financial mismanagement also results in lost potential, misery, disappointment, depression, and an inability to have a significant influence on the lives of others.

This certainly was true for us. Every time we wanted to pursue a dream, we were held back by financial commitments made in the past. We were also subject to all the swings and bubbles in the national economy.

I was puzzled that some people could prosper and enjoy life whether the global economy was good or bad. What was their secret? We made it our quest to find out.

Solomon, the wealthiest man who ever lived, said this: "Wisdom is supreme, therefore get wisdom. Though it cost all you have, get understanding" (Proverbs 4:7).

THE TRUTH WILL SET YOU FREE

Your thinking controls your success or failure in life. Your actions will follow what you truly believe.

If you truly *believe* you should be poor—or you *believe* you have no control over your economic circumstances—your mental perception will produce corresponding actions that result in poverty and lack.

The same is true if you *believe* you're not smart enough to compete. Your thought process will produce corresponding behavior, and that behavior will inevitably create a reality that corresponds to your thinking. This principle is time-tested and taken right from Scripture:

"As he thinks in his heart, so is he." —**Proverbs 23:7**

So why do individuals, communities and nations experience poverty and lack while others prosper? One of the primary reasons is that they have incorrect mindsets and attitudes about economic principles. The basic principles of finance and economics are not being taught in our schools. Instead, we are being shaped and programmed by marketing messages that run contrary to sound economics—influencing us to *violate* spiritual principles without even knowing it!

Our financial choices have *consequences*! Because of financial illiteracy, many people have been lulled into a way of thinking that will keep them in debt and financial bondage their entire lifetime.

REPROGRAM YOUR THINKING

The good news is that it's not too late to reprogram our thinking! As we study, and apply time-tested financial principles, our mindset will change, which will bring about prosperity instead of poverty.

Often we aren't even aware of how counterproductive and negative our thoughts and words have impacted our circumstances. For example, instead of focusing on the negative mindset that says, "I can't afford this or that," we must learn to ask the question, "What can I do to receive the resources needed to accomplish my objective?"

Never forget:

**THERE IS NO SHORTAGE OF MONEY IN THE WORLD
FOR THOSE WHOUNDERSTAND THE PRINCIPLES OF
INCREASE AND MULTIPLICATION.**

To create financial freedom, you must reeducate yourself and reprogram your mind. Your economic future depends on your ability to think for yourself and act on time-tested financial principles. According to God's Word, a line has been drawn in the sand as far as your financial future is concerned. On the one side is blessings and abundance, and on the other side is poverty and lack. The choice is yours.

THE KEYS TO TRANSFORMING YOUR FUTURE

Understanding that your financial future begins with a transformed mind is only the beginning. Also see what the Bible says about your economic birthright as a child of God, understanding that He has called you to a life filled with prosperity and abundance rather than poverty and lack.

Just as you have a spiritual destiny to be conformed to the image of Christ (Romans 8:29), you have an economic destiny to be blessed so you can be a blessing to others (Genesis 12:2). Just as God promises you spiritual or eternal blessings in Christ (Ephesians 1:3), He also promises to meet *all* your needs. (Philippians 4:19).

You see, you were created for a divine purpose. You have an assignment to fulfill, and that includes more than going to school, getting a job, paying your bills, and surviving. God wants you to use your unique gifts and talents to manage the resources He's entrusted to your care. The bigger your assignment, the more resources you will need. The better you manage your resources, the more resources you will be given to manage. Understanding this key will unlock your economic potential so you can fulfill your God-given assignment and destiny.

Once you grasp the great truth that God has a unique purpose for your life, He will unfold His specific instructions for how to reach that destiny.

IMAGINE WHAT IS POSSIBLE

God's plans for your future are more wonderful than you could ever imagine. The apostle Paul wrote that God "is able to do immeasurably more than all we ask or imagine, according to his power that is at work within us" (Ephesians 3:20 NIV).

It's time to start imagining what your financial future can look like if you put God in charge by following His principles...

- Imagine never having to struggle financially again, regardless of the economic conditions around you.

- Imagine not only having the financial resources you need to take care of your family, but also a surplus to help others.

- Imagine being a pipeline of blessings to those who are widows, orphans, homeless, or victims of natural disasters around the world.

- Imagine being so blessed that you can be a lender rather than a borrower, the head instead of the tail.

- Imagine having an estate that will continue to bless others well after you have left this earth.

This is just a small glimpse of what God has promised to those who act on His economic principles. No matter what your financial circumstances may be at this time, your financial turnaround can start today!

Notice what Abraham's servant said about the legacy Abraham was leaving for his son Isaac:

> **The LORD has blessed my master abundantly, and he has become wealthy. He has given him sheep and cattle, silver and gold, menservants and maidservants, and camels and donkeys. My master's wife Sarah has borne him a son in her old age, and he has given him everything he owns (Genesis 24:35-36 NIV).**

Abraham not only had a spiritual inheritance; he also had a surplus of wealth to leave a financial legacy to his family. Your economic success is a very important part of God's overall plan to demonstrate His covenant and promises to you: "You shall remember the LORD your God, for it is He who gives you power to get wealth, that He may establish His covenant" (Deuteronomy 8:18).

This scripture clearly points out that God wants to bless you financially, giving you "power to get wealth." This is one of the ways He shows the world His covenant faithfulness to His people. But of course, financial abundance is only *one* of His covenant blessings. He also wants to bless you spiritually, physically, emotionally and socially.

LEAVING A FINANCIAL LEGACY

God wants to give you a surplus lifestyle, with more than enough resources to meet your needs and enough left over to help meet the needs of others.

God has promised to be a source of blessings and wealth to those who follow His principles. These blessings are meant to be so abundant that they overflow into a financial legacy for future generations:

Blessed is the man who fears the LORD, Who delights greatly in His commandments.

His descendants will be mighty on earth; The generation of the upright will be blessed.

Wealth and riches will be in his house, And his righteousness endures forever (Psalm 112:1-3).

Is this the kind of spiritual and economic inheritance you are building for your children and grandchildren?

It was never planned for you to experience a life of constant financial struggles. If you've grown accustomed to living paycheck to paycheck, begging for a miracle every month just to cover your monthly bills and the minimum payments on your credit cards, I have surprising news for you: *You're settling for less than God's best!*

God has a better path for His people! Deuteronomy 28 summarizes many of His promises regarding the economic destiny you can have if you follow His instructions. Although this list is not all-inclusive, there are 10 specific blessings promised in this chapter as it relates to your economic destiny:

10 BLESSINGS GOD PROMISES YOU IN DEUTERONOMY 28

1. You will be blessed wherever you live, in the city or in the country (v. 3).

2. Your children will be blessed (v. 4).

3. Your finances will increase in your job or business (v. 4).

4. You will be blessed with an abundance of food (v. 5).

5. God will fight your battles and protect you from your enemies (v. 7).

6. Your storehouses will be blessed, increasing your bank accounts, savings and investments (v. 8).

7. Your success will be a testimony of God's blessings in your life (v. 10).

8. Because you've been a faithful steward of what you've received, God will bless your future generations (v. 11).

9. Instead of being in debt, you will be the lender and not the borrower (v. 12).

10. You will be the head and not the tail—having a position of influence and authority rather than servitude and lack (v. 13).

The ancient promises from God are remarkably relevant to our lives today. In addition to speaking of abundance in general terms, this passage specifically says the Lord wants us to be lenders instead of borrowers. Think of it: Long before anyone invented credit cards or subprime mortgages, God declared His desire to keep His people free from the bondage of debt!

ECONOMIC LAWS THAT GOVERN WEALTH

The promises outlined in Deuteronomy 28 are not automatic but *conditional*—based on our faithfulness to apply God's economic laws of prosperity. The Economic Destiny Program shares these vital principles for eliminating debt and gaining wealth:

KEY FINANCIAL PRINCIPLES OF THE ECONOMIC DESTINY PROGRAM

- **FINANCIAL PROSPERITY AND ABUNDANCE:** God has well-established principles that govern financial success. God has an *economic* plan for your life, just like He has a *spiritual* plan.

- **A LEGACY FOR FUTURE GENERATIONS:** Not only can you and your children be blessed, but you can also leave a legacy of success and prosperity for future generations.

- **FINANCIAL SURPLUS:** Your economic destiny is success and abundance. In addition to taking care of your family, you can have enough resources left over to give generously to others in your community and beyond.

- **FREEDOM FROM THE BONDAGE OF DEBT:** Your goal is to reposition yourself to be the lender and not the borrower. God wants you to be free from any encumbrances that distract you from His purpose and destiny for your life.

- **INCREASE AND MULTIPLICATION:** A natural outcome of your good stewardship will cause the growth of your financial assets. God has promised His blessing on your land and real estate, which shows that you have the right to homeownership and real estate investments.

- **BUSINESS OWNERSHIP:** A bi-product of good stewardship is industriousness and vision—and these are the key ingredients of personal entrepreneurship. When you properly manage the financial resources entrusted to your care, your business and investments will flourish.

- **FREEDOM FROM POVERTY AND LACK:** God wants to deliver you from a spirit of poverty and make you a source of blessings to your family and the people around you.

- **LEADERSHIP:** God wants you to be in a position of influence and authority—He will teach you to exercise this authority with integrity.

- **A GOOD NAME:** Live a life of honesty and integrity and you will have a good testimony in the community. People around you will see your success and listen to your counsel.

- **A GIVER:** Be a source of blessing to others. God will make you a distribution center of His love, a visible testimony of His favor. Because you are a giver and not a taker, people around you will be blessed by your surplus.

As you read these scriptural principles, can you see where you might have misinterpreted God's teachings about money? For example, I erroneously believed we should live "one day at a time" and not plan too far ahead or store up wealth for the future. I thought God would take care of me despite my lack of planning and preparation.

Although this may sound like a very "spiritual" philosophy, it doesn't work! To my dismay, I discovered that in my attempt to simply "trust God," I was naïve to the fact that I was violating many of His financial principles. Once I put my priorities in order and took control of my finances through sound financial stewardship, God began to bless me in ways I never imagined possible.

The same can be true for you. Your financial struggles can be a thing of the past! You're about to learn a simple plan that has helped thousands eliminate debt and achieve financial independence—regardless of income level or the conditions of our national economy.

KEY PRINCIPLE: GOD HAS A PURPOSE AND DESTINY FOR YOUR LIFE, AND THAT PURPOSE IS MUCH MORE IMPORTANT THAN MONEY. HE GIVES YOU MONEY TO EMPOWER YOU TO COMPLETE YOUR ASSIGNMENT AND IMPACT THE LIVES OF OTHERS.

No matter what your calling or career path, it's essential to learn how to properly manage money in order to be successful. Some were created to be business and community leaders, doctors, teachers, lawyers, broadcasters, inventors, politicians, writers, factory workers, small business owners, etc. Regardless of your profession, we all must learn to properly manage the money we earn.

KEY PRINCIPLE: GOD HAS PROVIDED YOU WITH THE GIFTS AND ABILITIES NEEDED TO SUCCESSFULLY FULFILL HIS PURPOSE FOR YOUR LIFE, REGARDLESS OF YOUR CIRCUMSTANCES OR WHAT IS HAPPENING IN THE ECONOMY.

God has given us well-defined principles to govern our economic affairs, and you'll find that it's simpler than you think to manage your money and build wealth. Remember that God has already established the legal parameters of our economic inheritance. The conditions are clearly defined in His Word—and the rest is up to you!

THE SEVEN KEY PRINCIPLES OF THE ECONOMIC DESTINY PROGRAM

The Economic Destiny Program has seven principles for achieving financial independence:

1. Planning to Prosper
2. Preparing for Rain
3. Stewardship in Action
4. Freedom from bondage
5. Turning waste into wealth
6. The Wise Investor
7. Leaving a Legacy

By applying the seven principles of the Economic Destiny Program, you can eliminate debt, systematically build long-term wealth, and leave a financial legacy regardless of the amount of income you earn. The next step is to develop a plan of action that corresponds with the application of these principles to your specific circumstances.

This is not going to be difficult. Built into the program are some cutting-edge tools and strategies that will be like having a financial GPS to effortlessly guide you in fulfilling your goals and arriving at your destination: *economic freedom*. Instead of taking years of futile striving to achieve financial independence, you'll be able to do it quickly and easily. Best of all, you can set your plan on autopilot.

Don't think I'm advocating some kind of get-rich-quick scheme. The Economic Destiny Program is based upon sound principles for achieving financial abundance. Instead of being "easy come, easy go," wealth created in this way is more likely to be here to stay.

We're going to start laying the foundation in the next chapter, so let's get started!

Chapter 8

THE POWER OF A PLAN
ECONOMIC DESTINY PRINCIPLE #1—
PLANNING AND PREPARATION

"Good fortune is what happens when opportunity meets
with planning and preparation." —Thomas Edison

"A man with a surplus can control his circumstances, but a man
without a surplus is controlled by them, and often has no
opportunity to exercise judgment" —Harvey S. Firestone

NOW THAT WE'VE LAID THE FOUNDATION for the principles of the Economic Destiny Program, we are ready to begin applying the first principle. I've created a lesson plan to help guide you through the process. It's broken into seven parts, corresponding to the seven principles of the Economic Destiny Program. In addition to the principles, we will also discuss practical action steps you can take to implement the principles and fulfill your long-term financial objectives.

The seven principles are the same for everyone, and they will transform your finances no matter what your present economic condition may be. I recognize that each individual is different, but

God's financial principles never change. Each individual has unique dreams they would like to see come to pass, and most of these desires have been placed in our heart by God. In order to arrive at our intended destination, we must understand the principle of planning and why it is an important part of long-term financial success.

THE POWER OF A PLAN

Planning ahead gives you the ability to look into the future and see your God-given dreams and destiny fulfilled. It helps you close the gap between hope and reality. And it's the natural bridge that carries you from where you are in the present to where you want to be in the future.

Let's look at these examples of people who have overcome difficulties and hardships to achieve amazing financial outcomes in their lives.

- A 76-year-old factory worker with less than a high school education overcame poverty and donated over $500,000 to his local church and other charities.

- A divorcee living in government housing was able to get off of welfare and purchase a nice home in the suburbs—and she completely paid off her home in less than seven years.

- A young secretary with two children who lost her job was able to live comfortably on her surplus for over 12 months while starting her own home-based business.

How were these people able to prosper, while those around them continued to settle for poverty and lack? These three people all had one thing in common—something many people choose to ignore: In addition to having a desire, they also had a *plan of action* that allowed them to accomplish their goals. Not only did they have a dream, but they also had the self-discipline to stick to their plan until they reached their objective. In addition, all of these individuals recognized the important role that having a surplus plays in the accomplishment of their objectives and included that as a key part of their plans.

ACTION STEP: PUT YOUR PLANS IN WRITING AND KEEP YOUR VISION BEFORE YOUR EYES, EVEN IN THE FACE OF SETBACKS AND ADVERSITY.

The difference between success and failure in a person's life usually centers around four vital ingredients:

1. A clear set of goals and objectives

2. A simple plan of action that fits their life circumstances

3. The discipline to consistently take small steps toward their goals

4. Knowing how to properly manage their existing income so they have a surplus—no matter how large or small the amount

ACTION STEP: AFTER YOU HAVE PUT YOUR GOALS IN WRITING, YOU MUST START TAKING SMALL STEPS IN THE DIRECTION OF YOUR GOALS UNTIL THEY ARE ACCOMPLISHED.

The purpose of this chapter is to help you organize a plan of action that enables you to walk in your full economic potential. By planning ahead, you can position yourself to accomplish what God's Word says you can accomplish. This is especially true when it comes to your personal finances.

Traditional financial planning has an objective: to get you to invest 5 to 10% of your monthly income in their investment products. However, *effective* financial planning has a completely different approach, taking into consideration your *entire* cash flow, not just a small portion of your income. By managing your whole dollar instead of just a part, you will get the maximum benefit from your income and be on the pathway toward achieving your long-term financial objectives.

OVERCOMING FINANCIAL LACK

"The trouble with many plans is that they are based on the way things are now. To be successful, your plan must focus on what you want in the future not what you have now." —Nido Qubein

To break the spirit of financial lack and get started on the road to economic freedom described in the Economic Destiny Program, it's imperative that you build a financial surplus. You must set a goal to spend less than you earn to maintain a surplus.

As mentioned in the previous chapter, the current financial statistics concerning American families are bleak. But are these the outcomes the families planned for? No, these are the outcomes they received because they did not *have* a plan! By carefully planning ahead, they could have systematically produces their desired results.

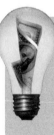

ACTION STEP: ORGANIZE YOUR FINANCIAL PLAN WITH SPECIFIC OUTCOMES AND OBJECTIVES THAT YOU WOULD LIKE TO ACCOMPLISH IN THE FUTURE. DON'T LEAVE YOUR DREAMS UP TO CHANCE OR RANDOM CIRCUMSTANCES.

Regardless of the economic circumstances around you, God wants you to position yourself to be a good testimony of His blessings in your life. But it's not enough for you simply to know God wants to bless you financially, you must also take the action steps necessary to receive His promised blessings.

TIME-TESTED PRINCIPLES FOR FINANCIAL SUCCESS

What does God say about planning ahead? The following scriptures provide some insights regarding the need to plan and prepare for your financial success:

Any enterprise is built by wise planning, becomes strong through common sense, and profits wonderfully by keeping abreast of the facts (Proverbs 24:3-5 TLB).

Suppose one of you wants to build a tower. Will he not first sit down and estimate the cost to see if he has enough money to complete it? (Luke 14:28 NIV)

A prudent man foresees difficulties ahead and prepares for them, the simpleton goes blindly on and suffers the consequence. Proverbs 22:3 (LBT)

A wise man saves for the future but a foolish man spends whatever he gets (Proverbs 21:20 TLB).

Write the vision; make it plain on tablets, so he may run who reads it (Habakkuk 2:2 ESV).

All of these verses make it clear that "wise planning" is an important foundation for a successful future. And for planning to have the maximum benefit, we should write down our plans in very specific details.

GOD'S PLAN FOR LONG-TERM FINANCIAL SUCCESS

From God's prospective, what are some of the things you should plan for? Notice the following passages.

Honor the LORD with your substance [wealth], with the first fruits of all your increase; then your barns will be filled with plenty, and your vats will overflow with new wine (Proverbs 3:9-10).

"Bring the whole tithe into the storehouse, so that there may be food in My house, and test Me now in this," says the LORD of hosts, "if I will not open for you the windows of heaven, and pour out for you a blessing until it overflows" (Malachi 3:10).

Now therefore, let Pharaoh select a discerning and wise man, and set him over the land of Egypt. Let Pharaoh do this,

and let him appoint officers over the land, to collect one-fifth [20%] of the increase of the land of Egypt in the seven years of plentiful (Genesis 41:32-34).

To take control of your finances, you must look at your total income from a different perspective. You must take control of each dollar and tell it which direction it should go. Do not leave its destination up to chance. Based on these passages, God's ideal financial plan to bless you in any economic season should look something like this:

FIGURE 1.0

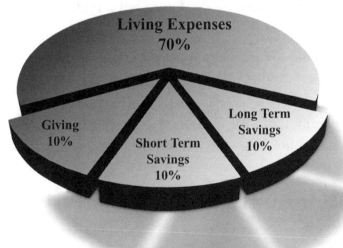

The "10/20/70 Rule": In addition to meeting your personal needs and living expenses, your plan should also include two other major components: giving and saving.

ACTION STEP: REALIZE THAT GOD HAS WELL ESTABLISHED PRINCIPLES THAT GOVERN FINANCIAL AND ECONOMIC SUCCESS. ORGANIZE YOUR FINANCIAL PLAN IN LINE WITH THE BLESSINGS THAT GOD HAS PROMISED.

As a steward, we are responsible for managing 100% of every dollar that has been entrusted to our care. We must revise our thinking to take into account that we are stewards over all the resources that God has given us.

Your objective here is to learn to live on 70% of your take home pay: 10% for giving, 20% for savings and 70% to cover living expenses. Although you may not be in a position to do this at the present time, I will walk you through the process so that it quickly becomes a reality.

ACTION STEP: TO TAKE CONTROL OF YOUR ECONOMIC DESTINY YOU MUST PLAN AHEAD AND ALLOCATE EACH DOLLAR TO WHERE YOU WANT IT TO GO.

PUTTING YOUR PLAN IN WRITING

Your goals should be consistent with God's expectations for our lives. In the last chapter, we discussed some specific outcomes that were promised in Deuteronomy 28 and are available to you if you are willing to put God's principles in operation. The Deuteronomy 28 promises are a covenant between you and God and they represent the major parts of your economic inheritance and should be included when setting your economic destiny goals.

You must organize your financial plan and set goals according to Biblical guidelines. From a practical perspective, here are some of the goals and outcomes you should include in your plan:

- Overflow and abundance—a financial surplus to share with others in need

- Freedom from the bondage of debt—positioning yourself to be the lender and not the borrower

- Leaving a financial legacy for your family and future generations

- Freedom from poverty and lack

- Real estate and homeownership

- Leadership and authority—becoming the head and not the tail

- A good name—being a good witness and good testimony to others

No matter what your present financial situation may be, listed here are some long-range financial goals built into the Economic Destiny Program that should be added to your economic destiny plan:

1. NO personal, unsecured debt (credit card, revolving accounts etc.)

2. NO car loans (unless self-financed through your own *Privatized Banking System "IBC"*) discussed in Chapter 14.

3. Own your home free and clear (a plan to pay off your mortgage within 5 to 7 years) using a mortgage acceleration software as your financial management system (page 40-41)

4. Tax-free income for retirement (drawn monthly/annually from your *"IBC"* plan)

5. A financial legacy goal for blessing your family and others

ACTION STEP: ALWAYS ORGANIZE YOUR FINANCIAL PLANS TO INCLUDE THE FINANCIAL DESTINY GOALS PROMISED IN GOD'S WORD.

In order to successfully complete God's assignment for your life, you must learn how to properly manage your financial resources and obligations. Although some of the specifics may vary from person to person, there are general stewardship principles which govern economic success *regardless* of your profession, family size, or income level.

IMPLEMENTING YOUR ECONOMIC DESTINY PLAN

So what are the practical steps you should take to accomplish these goals? First, you must determine where you are financially and develop a plan of action to take you from where are at *"the present"* to where you would like to be in *"the future."*

There are 3 primary steps you must take in order to implement your long-term financial goals:

1. GET AN ACCURATE ASSESSMENT OF YOUR CURRENT FINANCIAL CONDITION. This includes a realistic estimate of your current living expenses, starting with your existing cash flow: i.e., how much you earn versus how much you spend. (You can find a free financial analysis worksheet to help you in this process at **www.youreconomicdestiny.org**.

2. LIST YOUR FINANCIAL GOALS. You must have a clear vision of where you want to be in the future (one, five, 10, 20 and 30 years from now).

3. PUT YOUR PLAN IN WRITING. Writing down your financial goals is important to your long-range success. Keep your goals in a safe place and refer back to them often to see if you're closer or further away from achieving them.

ACTION STEP: ORGANIZE YOUR PLAN TO TAKE CONTROL OF EACH DOLLAR AND ALLOCATE IT TO WHERE IT MUST GO—NOT LEAVING ITS DIRECTION OR DESTINATION TO CHANCE.

REMEMBER: Statistics show that the average American family has no savings and spends 100% or more of their money without ever realizing it! Once their paycheck is spent, another paycheck comes, and they start the whole process all over again.

Think about that. A huge amount of money flows through their hands during their lifetime. Yet they never stop to ask how they could have changed the direction of that money, so it would flow back into their life rather than always flowing away from them.

In the next chapter, you will learn how to put an end to this fruitless cycle so you can reach your goals with certainty and precision. However, this is unlikely to happen unless you put your plans on autopilot. This is why the Economic Destiny Program works so well: You're more likely to reach your intended goals, because you're following the right plan and have the right tools to put those plans on autopilot.

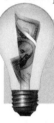

ACTION STEP: SET A GOAL TO GIVE 10% OF YOUR INCOME TO IMPACT THE LIVES OF OTHERS.

The following chart shows how the average person is currently budgeting their expenses if they are already giving 10% of their income. Giving is a major component to achieving financial success, and that is why an entire chapter is dedicated to that subject.

FIGURE 2.0 – OUTGOING EXPENDITURES VS. YOUR ENTIRE INCOME

Before

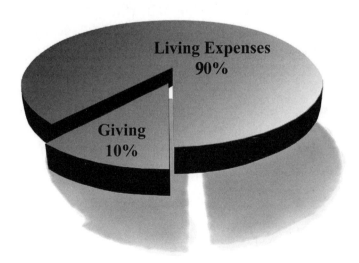

You might already be giving 10% of your income. Does that ensure that the other 90% is automatically going to be blessed? Not necessarily. Stewardship over *100%* of the income you receive is necessary in order to receive the full economic inheritance God intends for you.

Notice the illustration on the previous page for outgoing expenditures as they relate to 100% of your income. This is the amount of money you have to spend each month.

Most individuals spend 100% of their money without taking God's principles into account. If every individual gives 10% of their income to charitable organizations, this would be represented by the 10% shown in **Figure 2.0**. The 90% portion of **Figure 2.0** represents what they have left to cover all other expenditures (living expenses). The whole pie represents the total amount of income they earn.

GOAL: LIVE ON 70% OF YOUR INCOME

KEY PRINCIPLE: IT'S NOT HOW MUCH MONEY YOU EARN THAT COUNTS, IT'S HOW MUCH YOU KEEP. YOU MUST PROPERLY MANAGE WHAT YOU HAVE IN ORDER TO RECEIVE MORE.

ACTION STEP: IDENTIFY WHERE YOU ARE NOW AND WHERE YOU WANT TO BE IN THE FUTURE.

The Economic Destiny Program recommends that you set a goal to live on no more than 70% of your income. This goal might seem far-fetched if you've been living from paycheck to paycheck.

But let's consider the impact it would have if you realigned your finances to spend only 70% of each paycheck. What would this do for your personal finances? It would put you in a position to systematically accomplish every financial outcome outlined in the Economic Destiny Program.

Under this new arrangement, your outgoing expense chart would look like **Figure 3.0**:

FIGURE 3.0

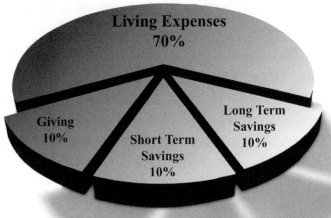

After giving the first 10% of each paycheck, set aside the next 20% of your income in surplus accounts. The remaining 70% would be available to spend on monthly living expenses.

Under this plan, you automatically force your monthly expenditures to line up with your long-term financial goals. The 10/20/70 structure will position you to receive all of the outcomes that God has promised in Deuteronomy 28.

ACTION STEP: BY SETTING FINANCIAL GOALS, ESTABLISHING A BUDGET, AND PLANNING AHEAD, YOU CAN GREATLY INCREASE BOTH YOUR PEACE OF MIND AND YOUR DISPOSABLE INCOME!

WHAT TO DO WITH THE 20%

Learning what to do with the 20% is an important key to receiving wealth and abundance. Proverbs 3:9 says: "Honor the Lord with your wealth and with the first fruit of your increase." Notice that this verse describes two separate and independent issues: wealth and increase. It's important that you understand the difference.

In some translations, the word wealth is translated "substance." Substance is your surplus or overflow—the 20% you should have left over after expenses.

The word for increase represents the income you receive. So this passage is saying to honor God with your substance (accumulated surplus or overflow) *and* your income. But you cannot fulfill this principle unless you *have* a surplus. Your "surplus" (not your income) will determine the amount of wealth you will accumulate over time.

How should this 20% surplus be appropriated? Make it your goal to set aside 10% in an account for short-term savings. This will provide you with a surplus account that can be used for emergencies, instead of reaching for the credit card to fill the gaps.

Having a surplus means you can plant seeds wherever there are needs and still have enough money to purchase the things you and your family need. You will also have enough resources to carry you through unforeseen events, repairs, medical bills, insurance deductibles, etc. And you will be able to pay cash for purchases instead of using credit cards and other unsecured revolving accounts.

Now take the next step and set aside another 10% of your net income for long-term savings.

ACTION STEP: SET A GOAL TO HAVE A MINIMUM OF SIX MONTHS OF LIVING EXPENSES IN YOUR SURPLUS ACCOUNT.

Imagine a debt-free life: zero mortgage debt, zero automobile loans, zero credit card debt or consumer debt of any kind. How would it feel to own your home free and clear, with no worries about the economic circumstances around you? Even if the world's economy is in a meltdown, you will have positioned yourself not only to survive, but to prosper.

NOTE: Setting aside 20% of your income and savings for surplus is a goal to shoot for. If you are not in a position to allocate 20% at the present time, at least set aside *something*. Start where you are and use what you have. Begin today by transferring some amount (even a few dollars) from your checking account to your short-term savings account.

As the old Persian proverb says, "A journey of 1,000 miles begins with one step." Small steps of faith will start you toward your goal of living on 70% of your income.

SUCCESS KEY: YOU MUST PREPARE YOURSELF FOR OPPORTUNITY BEFORE IT COMES. YOU RECEIVE TO THE EXTENT THAT YOU ARE PREPARED TO RECEIVE.

ACTION STEP: EDUCATE YOURSELF ON HOW MONEY WORKS, AND TAKE STEPS IN THE DIRECTION OF THE OUTCOMES YOU DESIRE.

In this chapter, we covered the principle of planning and preparation as it relates to your short and long-term financial success. The first step is determining where you are financially and developing a plan of action to take you from where are at the present to where you would like to be in the future.

If you are serious about getting your financial house in order and having the resources you need to bless the lives of others, your objective is to learn to live off of 70% of your take-home income.

If you can't envision how a plan like this is possible with your current income and obligations, then go to **www.youreconomicdestiny. org** and complete a free financial analysis. You will immediately see what is possible for you. This will remove your financial blind spots and give you a clear vision of the economic transformation you can begin to achieve.

In the next chapter, we're going to take a closer look at the power of surplus and how you can live an overflowing, abundant lifestyle regardless of your existing income. We will go into more detail on how to properly begin building a surplus by putting the accumulation process on *autopilot*!

Chapter 9 ——————————————————————
PREPARE FOR RAIN
ECONOMIC DESTINY PRINCIPLE #2 —
PAY YOURSELF FIRST AFTER GIVING BACK TO GOD

*"If virtue and knowledge are diffused among
the people, they will never be enslaved.
This will be their great security" —Samuel Adams 1779*

*"A wise man saves for the future, but a foolish man
spends whatever he gets." —Proverbs 21:20 (TLB)*

IN THE LAST CHAPTER, we discussed the role of proper planning in receiving our economic inheritance. If we're going to live in economic freedom and break the cycle of poverty in our lives, we must set goals and define specific steps that will carry us to our intended destination.

Now we are going to discuss how you can permanently break the spirit of lack and start living an overflow lifestyle. God's economy operates on the principle of surplus, and this is one of the most effective weapons against the spirit of poverty and lack. But you will never have a surplus unless you develop the habit of saving by creating automated systems and processes to "pay yourself first" (after giving back to God).

Money is a very powerful tool if it's put to work in the correct manner, yet people rarely understand how to do this. After many years in the financial services industry, it still bewildered me that most people accumulated very little wealth, no matter how much money they made. Even though they worked hard for many years to climb the income ladder, they found themselves unprepared for retirement or even the ordinary financial crises of life.

When these clients took an honest inventory of all their efforts to secure a better financial future for themselves and their family, they realized they were miles away from their intended destination: financial independence. They reflected on their years of hard work and long hours at the office to drive nicer cars or purchase a bigger house. Where had all their income gone?

When people do a thorough inventory of their cash flow, they're often startled to see how much of their income is flowing right through their hands to increased monthly payments on debts and unnecessary services—all to fund a lifestyle they feel they deserve because of the their hard work and income level.

WHERE DID THE MONEY GO?

I'm certainly not against having you enjoy the fruits of your labor and receiving nice things in your life. But you have to ask yourself a sobering question: After all these years of working hard to gain more wealth, why do your savings reflect only a fraction of what you could have accumulated?

What would happen if you had to stop working for some reason and your income stream dried up for a period of time? Could you survive for 6 months, 12 months, or longer and keep up with your same bills and economic lifestyle? Most people would struggle to maintain their current lifestyle for more than a month or two.

If this is your situation, I understand. I've been there myself. But the good news is that you don't have to remain in this precarious situation. If you follow the Economic Destiny Program, you won't have to continue living from paycheck to paycheck, just one unexpected bill from falling off the financial cliff.

In study after study, the savings rate for the average American family is below the 2nd percentile. According to a study by the University of North Dakota, 54% of Americans are broke by age of 65. This means more than half of all Americans will arrive at retirement age dependant on some form of government assistance just to meet their basic monthly needs.

This doesn't have to be your financial destiny! You shouldn't be looking to the government to save you, nor should you rely upon your financial planner to perfectly time the stock market just right and preserve your investments. Your only hope of achieving true independence and security is to build a surplus through a principle-centered money management lifestyle.

Building a surplus is about saving money you can't afford to lose in order to systematically grow an ever-increasing nest egg. This can only be accomplished when you learn and apply the principle of paying yourself first.

UNDERSTANDING THE OVERFLOW PRINCIPLE

One day while spending some time with one of my financial mentors, the topic of savings came up. To my surprise, he said that savings is a principle that will reap rewards, opportunities and success in *any* economic cycle. My attention hung on every word, as he proceeded: "Jeff, I've discovered the importance of the overflow principle, and this discovery has completely changed the way I manage the finances of my business." He explained that since his business depended on the sale of products and services, the overflow principle was a crucial step in helping him succeed even amid fluctuations in the market.

This made perfect sense to me. If a business spends its entire income each month, what will it do when it runs into an emergency? But if a business has sufficient reserves, that buffer can mean the difference between success and failure in the event of an unexpected emergency or drop in income. This discovery has application to both business and personal finances, and it's a critical step on the pathway toward financial independence.

Most people depend on the bank to be their business partner, always there when they run into trouble and need help. But what if interest rates increase and credit lines are reduced? Or what if there's a downturn in the economy and sales fall below expectations?

Neither a business nor a family can enjoy long-term financial stability and success without a surplus account. God made the overflow principle a major part of His economic system, and those who are wise will faithfully apply it and experience success.

SEEDTIME AND HARVEST

The Bible often describes its precepts in agrarian terms, such as "seedtime and harvest" (Genesis 8:22). We're repeatedly told that it's vitally important to set aside a portion of our harvest for the "winter" season that is coming, and that we must regularly sow additional seeds in anticipation of our next harvest.

Even the ants instinctively follow this pattern:

> **Go to the ant, you sluggard; consider its ways and be wise! It has no commander, no overseer or ruler, yet it stores its provisions in summer and gathers its food at harvest (6:6-8 NIV).**

Just as there are seasons in nature, there are economic seasons as well. If you are earning an income—no matter how large or small—you are currently in your summer. Having a surplus left over from your summer harvest provides you with a critical cushion for the winter seasons that will come.

Just as we shouldn't be shocked when winter comes, neither should we claim surprise when financial storms come our way. God tells us there *inevitably* will be such seasons in the world economy and our personal lives, so we had better prepare for them!

Most small businesses fail in their first 24 months, usually because they had insufficient reserves. Often they became dependent on SBA loans and bank credit lines to help them bridge the inevitable seasons and cycles their business would face. As a result, they fell into a terrible trap: believing they had to go deeper and deeper into debt in order to make a future profit.

In contrast, God's Word says to prepare for life's seasons and storms by preparing, counting the cost, and storing up reserves from your harvests. Building a surplus provides the peace of mind of knowing we are prepared for unexpected circumstances or emergencies. In addition, the surplus provides the resources we need to access new business opportunities and be ready in any season to bless the lives of others.

Instead of heeding these powerful lessons of seedtime and harvest, many Americans today are modeling the folly of spending everything they earn: "The wise man saves for the future, but the foolish man spends whatever he gets" (Proverbs 21:20 TLB). No wonder bankruptcies and foreclosures are happening at a record pace. Yes, our nation has faced some difficult economic storms the past few years, but those who were wise prepared ahead of time and had a surplus.

The principle of seedtime and harvest not only applies to personal and business finances, but it also applies and works in the management of a national economy. In Genesis 41, Joseph used this principle to change the destiny of an entire nation:

> **Let Pharaoh select a discerning and wise man, and set him over the land of Egypt.**
>
> **Let Pharaoh do this, and let him appoint officers over the land, to collect one-fifth [20%] of the produce of the land of Egypt in the seven plentiful years.**
>
> **And let them gather all the food of those good years that are coming, and store up grain under the authority of Pharaoh, and let them keep food in the cities.**
>
> **Then that food shall be as a reserve for the land for the seven years of famine which shall be in the land of Egypt, that the land may not perish during the famine (Genesis 41:33-36).**

Are you saving a "reserve" during *your* "plentiful years" or months? If so, you'll have nothing to worry about during any "years of famine" that shall come.

This is something that's difficult for most people. Without a plan, it simply won't happen. That is why you must understand and employ Principle #2 of the Economic Destiny Program: Pay Yourself First.

YOUR PATHWAY TO FINANCIAL ABUNDANCE

REMEMBER: God has a purpose and destiny for your life. But you will never move beyond the limits of your present financial circumstances until you change your thinking about money and savings. One of my reasons for writing this book is to help you examine your attitudes and perspectives to see if your actions are being controlled by a poverty mindset.

God says He wants you to have a life of overflowing abundance:

Honor the LORD with your substance [wealth], with the first fruits of all your increase; then your barns will be filled with plenty, and your vats will overflow with new wine (Proverbs 3:9-10).

Notice that you cannot honor God and follow the instructions of this passage unless you have "substance" (a surplus). You gain wealth by accumulating substance (overflow) from the increase you receive over a period of time—as you consistently spend less than you earn.

KEY PRINCIPLE: IF YOU SPEND LESS THAN YOU EARN, YOU WILL ALWAYS HAVE A SURPLUS.

Financial increase is a natural byproduct of following God's economic plan. An important part of that plan is building a surplus. When you have a surplus, you're in a position to fulfill all the requirements necessary to receive the blessings/outcomes God promised as your inheritance in Deuteronomy 28. And you'll not only be able to honor the Lord with your substance, but you'll also be in a position to dramatically impact the lives of others (relatives, friends, community, charitable organizations, etc.).

Your objective is to position yourself and your resources to have enough left over to develop your substance/surplus account. This is the KEY to your long-term financial success and your ability to give to God and others.

Give, and it will be given to you, good measure, pressed down, shaken together and running over, will be poured into your lap. For with the measure you use, it will be measured to you (Luke 6:38 NIV).

A generous man will prosper; he who refreshes others will himself be refreshed (Proverbs 11:25 NIV).

REMEMBER:

YOUR FINANCIAL SUCCESS IN LIFE IS NOT DETERMINED BY HOW MUCH MONEY YOU EARN, BUT BY HOW MUCH YOU HAVE LEFT OVER TO IMPACT THE LIVES OF OTHERS.

Great opportunities are ahead if you position yourself to have a surplus! In addition to meeting others' needs without borrowing to do so, you'll be ready to take advantage of amazing investment opportunities that come your way.

Do a brief self-assessment today: Are you fulfilling God's purpose for your life by using your time, talent and treasure to leave the world a better place? Or are you consuming everything you earn, just to survive?

ACTION STEPS

The key to begin building wealth through a surplus is Economic Destiny Principle #2: Pay Yourself First. But although this is a simple principle to state, many people stumble over the needed action steps. In fact, most people pay themselves LAST, after all their other bills are paid. However, those who take this approach quickly discover that there's seldom anything left over to begin building their surplus account.

Unless you learn to apply the Pay Yourself First principle, you'll never find the pathway to financial independence. Instead of building a surplus, you'll end up encumbering your future earnings to pay for things you need today. But if you have a surplus, you can use cash for today's emergencies and then move into your future as a free citizen—never again enslaved and weighted down by your past financial decisions.

REMEMBER: The Economic Destiny Program is meant to be a *simple* plan for financial independence. So what can you do to end the dilemma of always having more month than you have money? How can you break the cycle of poverty and permanently change your financial circumstances—starting today?

Once you recognize that God wants you to be free from financial bondage so you can live an abundant life, some simple adjustments in your money management habits will enable you to get off the frustrating treadmill of spending everything you earn.

Your financial turnaround starts by taking these three action steps:

 **ACTION STEP 1:** REEXAMINE YOUR DECISION-MAKING PROCESSES, AND START MAKING CHOICES THAT ARE CONSISTENT WITH GOD'S SCRIPTURAL PRINCIPLES.

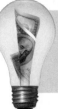 **ACTION STEP 2:** MAKE A FIRM COMMITMENT TO CHANGE ANY LIFESTYLE CHOICES THAT ARE PREVENTING YOU FROM LIVING IN GOD'S OVERFLOW.

 **ACTION STEP 3:** SET A GOAL TO PAY YOURSELF FIRST FROM EVERY PAYCHECK YOU RECEIVE. YOU CAN PUT THIS PROCESS ON AUTOPILOT BY FOLLOWING A FEW SIMPLE INSTRUCTIONS:

- Open a separate savings account to use for building your surplus.

- Instruct your employer's payroll department to automatically deposit a percentage of your paycheck into this surplus account.

- If your employer does not provide this service, then ask your bank to set up an automatic transfer of 10% to 20% into your surplus account the day after your auto-deposited paycheck goes into your checking account.

It's critical that you put the Pay Yourself First process on autopilot and have the money put into a separate account. Don't try to leave this to chance! A checking account is a spending account, and you're extremely unlikely to faithfully transfer a portion of your income into your surplus account every payday.

If you're like most people, every dollar that goes into your checking account will go right back out. This is true no matter how much money you earn. By having your savings come right off the top of your income, you will automatically begin to adjust your spending and build a surplus.

POWERFUL TOOLS TO HELP YOU

Many people ask me whether their checking account or online bill pay is the best way to track their spending. The answer is yes and no. Today there are software tools that have been developed for managing your finances with absolute precision. If you have any kind of debt at all, you will want to use these tools for managing your debt pay off and your monthly cash flow.

I'm now able to help my clients utilize easy-to-use software that allows them to track and manage every expenditure from a single place. This is like a GPS for their finances, enabling them to reach their intended financial destination on the most efficient path possible. Just as banks have all kinds of internal software to make sure their every dollar is working to its maximum potential, my clients are experiencing similar benefits as well.

Before I used these simple financial tools, I was only tracking my spending through my checking account. This pattern kept me from consistently building any savings, and I was also losing thousands of dollars in interest that I could not see. I thought I had no other choice.

Once I discovered how powerful these software tools were, I quickly realized why banks are so good at making *their* surplus work 24 hours a day, 7 days a week. I learned that money in the hands of a bank's computer never sleeps, and interest accumulation never takes a break. After applying these financial tools in my life and the lives of my clients, we're all having much more success in building and maintaining a surplus.

You can experience these same benefits! Even without the benefit of this amazing software, if you establish an automatic transfer of funds from your checking account into a savings account, you will be positioning yourself to build a surplus.

You will be much less likely to spend money you don't see in your checking account. Once you set this plan in motion and automatically have the funds transferred away from your checking account, you'll never miss the money. You will simply adjust your lifestyle to fit within what's left over in your spending account. Like taxes withheld on your pay stub, it's money you will never see, so you force yourself to live only on the remaining money.

Here are some additional tips to consider:

- Set up a separate account for giving—over and above the 10% you contribute to your church or favorite charity.

- When you take money from your short-term savings account for an emergency or any other purpose, always replace the amount you use before you make additional purchases. Your objective is to always have a minimum of three to six months of cash reserves in your emergency account, where you have easy access to the money.

- Good money management software is one of the best tools for reducing expenditures and interest payments so you can always have a reserve. Managing the flow of your money is just math, so let the software do the math for you. That way you can focus on what you do best and keep the income coming in on a consistent basis.

GETTING "RICH WITH LOANS"?

No one can fully see the future except God. In the Scriptures, He gave us specific instructions about saving a portion of everything we earn, because our circumstances and the economy will always undergo seasons and cycles. This is a profound and indisputable fact of life, yet it's overlooked by many people, including those who claim to believe the teachings of the Bible.

Even many economists today are foolishly saying our nation must "spend its way to a better economy." Isn't that philosophy a direct contradiction of God's economic principles? Yes it is, for any prosperity that comes from increasing our borrowing is only an illusion—*false* prosperity. In fact, Scripture ridicules those who make themselves "rich with loans" (Habakkuk 2:7 NASB). Instead of creating true wealth, that's a road that always leads to bondage.

When people fail to develop a surplus, they always end up using credit to pay for emergencies or bridge the gaps between economic cycles. Once they've established this habit, it's difficult to break. Eventually there's a tipping point, and the bondage becomes over-whelming. But all this could have been avoided if they had just taken time to plan ahead and build a surplus. That's the proven path to financial freedom.

Often the clients I coach ask me, "What about putting 10% in a 401(k) fund, particularly if my employer matches my contributions?" This is a great idea IF your employer matches your contributions, because this is like a 100% return. **BUT REMEMBER THIS:** A 401(k) plan is not a savings plan, but rather an investment plan. Accordingly, it is subject to risk, because your principal contributions are subject to unknown future tax rates and usually not protected from loss.

I tell my clients not to confuse *saving* with *investing*. They are two different animals and should not be mixed! We will discuss this in more detail later, and I also will explain the best places to grow your wealth.

The main thing to remember at this point is to make sure you have 3 to 6 months of living expenses in your short-term saving account, where you can have instant access in case of an emergency. In contrast, a 401(k) is a long-term investment vehicle that provides very limited access to your money until you reach retirement age. If you need the money in your 401(k) before age 59.5, you are subject to losing some of your principal due to penalties and taxes.

DON'T WAIT! START TODAY!

Sometimes people hear the "Pay Yourself First" message and tell me, "That's a great goal, Jeff. Someday I hope I'm in a position to do that."

This response misses a crucial point:

YOU SHOULD START WHERE YOU ARE, WITH THE FINANCIAL RESOURCES YOU HAVE, REGARDLESS OF YOUR CURRENT ECONOMIC SITUATION.

You don't have to wait until you're able to contribute a full 10% of your income to your surplus account. Start the process immediately, even if you are only able to deposit $10 per paycheck. Get started today! If you take this first step forward, you will begin to see the overflow principle take root in your life. You'll see God's blessings released, because you'll be acting on His principles of increase and multiplication.

Procrastination is not an option. You must understand that God's Word has drawn a line in the sand. On one side is blessing and abundance, and on the other side is the curse of poverty and lack. There is no gray area when it comes to benefiting from the steward-ship principle of seedtime and harvest.

EITHER YOU WILL ACT NOW AND HAVE INCREASE, OR YOU WILL DELAY AND EXPERIENCE DECREASE.

REVIEWING KEY PRINCIPLES

By using the Pay Yourself First principle, you can permanently break the spirit of poverty and get off of the financial treadmill of spending more than you earn. God wants you to have a lifestyle of overflowing abundance, but this means learning how to control your spending and develop a surplus. This can be done on your existing income, without seriously restricting your current lifestyle.

If you follow the strategies outlined in the Economic Destiny Program, building a surplus will become an automatic part of your financial plan. Based on the overflow principle, you will always have a surplus if you spend less than you earn. But instead of just living paycheck to paycheck, you must automatically save a portion of all your income—with an ultimate goal of setting aside 20% of your net take-home pay.

By establishing your surplus account, you prove that you're serious about getting your financial house in order. This vital first step will become the basis for accomplishing your long-term financial goals.

In the next chapter, we'll discuss how financial stewardship relates to managing your existing income. You'll be amazed by the rewards God promises to those who follow His economic plan.

Chapter 10

THE STEWARDSHIP PRINCIPLE
ECONOMIC DESTINY PRINCIPLE #3—
FINANCIAL STEWARDSHIP

"'The silver is Mine, and the gold is Mine,' says the LORD of hosts."
—Haggai 2:8

"You shall remember the LORD your God, for it is He who gives
you power to get wealth, that He may establish His covenant which
He swore to your fathers, as it is this day." —Deuteronomy 8:18

MANY PEOPLE ARE STRUGGLING to make ends meet. Although they have good incomes, they can't seem to hold on to what they earn.

In contrast, we've all met people who seem to be thriving, even though their incomes are barely above the poverty line. Somehow they're able to build more wealth than anyone would expect.

How could this be? Many people have adopted the fatalistic view that successful people have simply "won life's lottery" through no merit of their own. They assume God randomly chooses some people or nations to be rich and others to be poor. We have no responsibility at all. Financial abundance is just the luck of the draw.

But this is not what the Bible teaches! It says those who are "willing and obedient…shall eat the good of the land" (Isaiah 1:19). The outcomes we experience in life are largely the product of the *choices* we make. That means it's up to us which side of the rich/poor line we're on. By following scriptural principles, we can ensure that we have blessing and abundance rather than poverty and lack.

STEWARDSHIP IS THE KEY

Although the Bible mentions a number of factors that will either help us or hinder us in gaining wealth, the most important key is to understand and implement the principles of stewardship. This begins with a realization that God is the rightful owner of everything we have, and then the next step is learning to properly manage the time, talent, and financial resources He's entrusted to us.

Over the years I've been surprised to meet so many people who are completely ignorant of what the Bible says about stewardship. This is true even of many people who attend church regularly and claim to believe the Bible from cover to cover.

REMEMBER: Stewardship is no minor issue!

THE PRINCIPLE OF STEWARDSHIP IS SO FOUNDATIONAL THAT IT CAN COMPLETELY TRANSFORM A PERSON'S ECONOMIC DESTINY. THOSE WHO PROVE THEMSELVES TO BE GOOD STEWARDS WILL BE REWARDED ABUNDANTLY, BOTH IN THIS PRESENT LIFE AND IN THE LIFE TO COME!

KEY PRINCIPLE: THE BIBLE PROVIDES MANY INSIGHTS ABOUT GOD'S DESIRE TO BLESS US WITH ABUNDANCE, BUT FAITHFUL FINANCIAL STEWARDSHIP IS THE MOST IMPORTANT KEY OF ALL.

The English word "stewardship" comes from the Greek word *oikonomos*, which is the root for our word "economist." Dictionaries define a steward as one who manages another's property or financial affairs. A steward is morally responsible for the careful use of money, time, talents and other resources.

To be a good steward requires us to be a good "economist" with what we have. There is no exception to this rule. If we work for someone else, we're basically "business managers" of the sphere we've been entrusted with. Likewise, a homemaker is responsible for various economic decisions affecting the management of the household.

KEY PRINCIPLE: FAITHFULNESS BRINGS INCREASE. IT'S NOT HOW MUCH YOU HAVE THAT COUNTS, BUT HOW WELL YOU MANAGE WHAT YOU HAVE.

In order to grasp this principle in its entirety, we must understand that a steward's task is to manage someone else's resources in line with the owner's expectations. Before we can reap the blessings, benefits, and promises of our position, we must see that God is the owner of everything, and He has given us specific guidelines and authority to manage His resources:

> The earth is the LORD's, and everything in it, the world, and all who live in it (Psalm 24:1 NIV).

> Yours, O LORD, is the greatness, the power and the glory, the victory and the majesty; for all that is in heaven and in earth is Yours; Yours is the kingdom, O LORD, and You are exalted as head over all. Both riches and honor come from You, and You reign over all. In Your hand is power and might; in Your hand it is to make great and to give strength to all (1 Chronicles 29:11-12).

> Who then is that faithful and wise steward, whom his master will make ruler over his household...? (Luke 12:42)

It's impossible for a steward to be successful if he doesn't understand the owner's expectations. As stewards over His financial resources, God expects us to multiply His resources by reducing waste, decreasing liabilities, and increasing assets. If we faithfully manage His resources in line with these expectations, He will give us even more. People can become very successful in accomplishing their assignment in life just by properly managing the resources God has already given them.

So what are some wise guidelines for managing our income and expenses in line with God's expectations? The basic outline is this: 10% for giving, 10% for emergencies and leaner seasons, and 10% for long-term wealth-building. Then we must force our lifestyle and monthly expenses to fit within the remaining 70%. If we learn to live on 70% of our income, the long-term blessings of increase will be automatic.

EXPECT AN INCREASE!

The Bible makes it clear that a "good and faithful" steward will be given even *more* resources to manage:

> **So he who had received five talents came and brought five other talents, saying, "Lord, you delivered to me five talents; look, I have gained five more talents besides them." His lord said to him, "Well done, good and faithful servant; you were faithful over a few things, I will make you ruler over many things. Enter into the joy of your lord" (Matthew 25:20-21).**

Those who honor the Lord with their possessions are told, "Your barns will be **filled** with plenty, and your vats will **overflow** with new wine" (Proverbs 3:9-10). What a great promise!

GOD WANTS YOU TO BE FILLED TO OVERFLOWING, AND THIS STARTS WITH BEING A FAITHFUL STEWARD AND HONORING HIM WITH THE POSSESSIONS YOU ALREADY HAVE!

Too often, people make excuses for their impoverished lives. They think all their financial problems would disappear if only they were better educated...had wealthier parents...won the lottery...or got a raise at work. But they're failing to grasp a foundational key in God's economy:

THE WAY TO INCREASE THE AMOUNT OF RESOURCES IN YOUR LIFE IS TO START FAITHFULLY MANAGING WHAT YOU ALREADY HAVE. WHEN YOU LEARN TO BETTER MANAGE WHAT YOU HAVE, GOD WILL GIVE YOU MORE RESOURCES TO MANAGE.

KEY PRINCIPLE: BEING FAITHFUL WITH WHAT YOU HAVE IS A PREREQUISITE FOR GETTING MORE.

As you demonstrate your faithfulness with small amounts of money, doors will open to give you larger amounts to manage. If you don't properly manage a small income, how can you expect to be given a larger one?

Jesus summarized the stewardship principle this way:

"Whoever can be trusted with very little can also be trusted with much, and whoever is dishonest with very little will also be dishonest with much. So if you have not been trustworthy in handling worldly wealth, who will trust you with true riches? And if you have not been trustworthy with someone else's property, who will give you property of your own?" (Luke 16:10-12 NIV)

God wants to bless us with greater abundance—but we'll receive those blessings in proportion to our faithfulness as stewards over what He's already given us.

So the primary reason for a person's lack of success is not that they were lacking opportunity or received an inadequate education. Their success or failure will ultimately depend on their stewardship— the proper management of their time, talent and financial resources. Those who aren't faithful with the money they have will find it taken away and put in the hands of others (Matthew 25:28-29).

KEY PRINCIPLE: YOUR STEWARDSHIP COVERS EVERYTHING YOU DO WHILE HERE ON EARTH. IT NOT ONLY INCLUDES YOUR FINANCES, BUT ENCOMPASSES EVERY AREA OF YOUR LIFE. YOUR SUCCESS IN LIFE IS GOVERNED BY HOW WELL YOU MANAGE THESE VARIOUS AREAS.

The good news is that our success and failure in life is usually determined not by things beyond our control, but rather by things we CAN control—by the choices we make and how well we apply God's stewardship principles. If we don't realize a financial stewardship principle exists, or if we intentionally disregard it, the promised benefits won't be received.

If I sound like a preacher on this point, I guess you're right. **BUT REMEMBER:** Your *economic* destiny cannot be separated from your *spiritual* destiny. God *cares* about how you handle your money!

KEY PRINCIPLE: THERE IS A CLOSE RELATIONSHIP BETWEEN FAITHFULLY MANAGING YOUR FINANCES AND FAITHFULLY HANDLING SPIRITUAL THINGS.

DEAL WITH ROOT CAUSES

The Economic Destiny Program is designed to deal with the *root causes* that hold people back from financial health. Often these root issues are fairly simple to describe—yet they require you to make new choices to implement the principles of God's Word.

Sometimes people approach me in bewilderment about how they ever sunk so low into financial bondage. After listening to them for a while, I typically find myself telling them...

"INSTEAD OF BEING BEWILDERING, YOUR FINANCIAL PROBLEMS ACTUALLY STEM FROM A VERY BASIC ROOT CAUSE: *YOU ARE SPENDING BEYOND YOUR MEANS."*

In his book, *We Don't Die, We Kill Ourselves*, heart surgeon Dr. Cris Enrique states that people are dying unnecessarily, because they think they don't have any control over their physical health. Contrary to this common mindset, Dr. Enrique points out that the top 10 causes of death can be prevented or even reversed by simple changes in lifestyle habits. *Our attitudes and actions DO make a difference!*

Sadly, people's lack of knowledge often causes them to make the same mistakes over and over again. In many cases, their poor dietary habits have been passed down from generation to generation. But the root problem isn't genetic but simply a matter of poor choices.

Positive changes are possible in practically every area of our lives. In most cases, simple adjustments in our attitudes and lifestyle can dramatically improve our health and quality of life. Yet the predominant medical establishment is designed to keep people on medications that treat their symptoms, instead of truly addressing the root causes of their health problems.

It's the same way in the financial services industry: What you're offered by banks and lenders is usually presented as the only viable option. Meanwhile, the financial industry is making large sums of money dealing with your symptoms instead of offering solutions that actually address the root causes of your money problems.

In my financial coaching sessions, I point out to clients that many of the same principles in the medical field are true in the financial arena. I've found that many people suffer unnecessarily, not only from the inadequate products offered, but also because of their improper attitudes and spending habits.

Just as in the area of health, many people make the same financial mistakes again and again. Poor money management habits are passed down from one generation to another, and the results are very predictable. Unless people change their attitudes and take control of their spending, it won't matter how much money they earn.

Just as medicine only treats people's symptoms, most of the traditional financial products merely provide temporary, superficial relief of people's distress—failing to address the root causes of their long-term financial problems. Here are some examples of products that offer seductive, short-term relief, while usually resulting in even greater long-term economic bondage:

- Mortgage refinancing for a slightly lower monthly payment, while extending the term of the mortgage by many years

- Debt consolidation loans that create lower monthly payments for a while—until you max-out your credit cards all over again

- Pre-approved credit card offers with *temporary* low interest rates but then exorbitant rates once the trial period is over

- Investment advisors who place your money in the stock market and tell you that if you just diversify and hold long-term, you will beat the odds and come out with a profit down the road

- The government pushing 401(k)'s as a safe and productive place to earn tax-deferred income, when the truth is that people could do better by paying taxes on the smaller amount now ("the seed"), rather than paying taxes later on the larger amount ("the harvest")

These deceptive "solutions" are not solutions at all! They will never heal the problem, but are temporary, short-term fixes to help you feel more comfortable in your financial disease.

Don't be seduced into giving up an entire lifetime of freedom in exchange for feeling comfortable in your existing condition. You don't have to remain in bondage to a system that's designed to keep us financially sick.

CONSIDER YOUR WAYS

As a steward, realize that you will be held accountable for how you manage what God has given you. If you find yourself in financial bondage, you must ask God to show you the root of the problem. In most cases, He will tell you to "consider your ways" and set new priorities:

You have sown much, and bring in little; you eat, but do not have enough; you drink, but you are not filled with drink; you clothe yourselves, but no one is warm; and he who earns wages, earns wages to put into a bag with holes. Thus says the LORD of hosts: "Consider your ways!" (Haggai 1:6-7)

God expects you to have control over your financial circumstances, and His Word offers you the principles and knowledge to do just that. Perhaps your current financial situation is a lot like the people in Haggai's day: earning wages but putting them "into a bag with holes." If this is the case, you're reading the right book!

There's a remedy for your financial predicament. After we walk through all seven principles of the Economic Destiny Program, you'll be equipped to step into a new life of economic freedom.

THE BIGGEST HOLE IN YOUR ECONOMIC BASKET

The average American family spends about 35% to 45% of their annual income on interest payments—on items such as home mortgages, car loans, credit cards, and student loans. For most people, this overwhelming debt load is by far the largest hole in their budget.

If this is how *your* budget looks, notice the startling news in **Figure 4.0** on the next page: You're going *backwards* in your finances, unnecessarily losing money every year.

As this chart shows, the average American family is actually losing money even in their attempt to invest for their retirement. They're allowing 35% to 40% of their income to flow out of their lives and into the hands of someone else. This is an example of poor stewardship!

Notice in **Figure 4.0** that even though you may think your investments are growing, on one side of the equation you are losing more than you are gaining on the other side of the equation. In other words, you actually are *losing* money even when it appears you are getting a return on your investments. This is a shortsighted way to handle your money. Instead, you must have stewardship over every dollar, making it work to your advantage.

FIGURE 4.0

Your Household Earns a Net $100,000 Annual Income

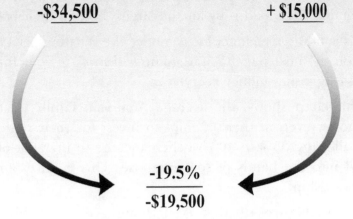

34.5%
Of Your Annual Income
Goes to Interest Payments

$150,000
In a Retirement Account
Earning a 10% Annual Return

-$34,500

+ $15,000

-19.5%
-$19,500
Your "real" Annual Return

REMEMBER...

YOU WILL NEVER SEE YOUR WEALTH INCREASE AND MULTIPLY IF YOUR MORTGAGE AND OTHER DEBTS CONTINUE TO CONSUME A LARGE PORTION OF YOUR MONTHLY INCOME.

To close the largest holes in your finances and start taking 100% stewardship over every dollar, you *must* get out of debt. Eliminating interest payments on debt will free up a considerable amount of money to devote to savings and investments. Interest payments—whether on your mortgage, credit cards, or some other form of debt—are an economic *killer*. They destroy your hopes and dreams and keep you from building a legacy for the next generation.

In the next chapter, I'll share more about the reality of living a debt-free lifestyle, along with tips for getting there fast—without having to live on rice and beans or drive clunker cars.

REGAINING FINANCIAL CONTROL

So how do you truly take control and have stewardship over your finances?

KEY PRINCIPLE: REMEMBER THAT INCOME IS NOT THE SAME AS WEALTH. INCOME IS ONLY YOUR POTENTIAL FOR BUILDING WEALTH. WEALTH IS THE ACCUMULATION OF ASSETS OVER A PERIOD OF TIME. IT'S THE PRODUCT OF GOOD STEWARDSHIP—THE PROPER MANAGEMENT OF THE RESOURCES THAT HAVE COME INTO YOUR POSSESSION.

BEGIN BY SPENDING WITHIN YOUR MEANS!

Spending within your means is a crucial element of good stewardship. But in order to spend within your means, you must take control of each dollar and allocate it in the direction it should go. The first step in this process is developing a budget—a critical foundation for your long-term wealth-building program.

A budget is a written or electronic plan that takes into account your existing circumstances and the direction you want your finances to go. It must show every source of income and every category of expenditure, including interest rates, terms and balances.

A budget is a plan of action that enables you to get the maximum benefits from your existing income. It causes you to set spending priorities in line with your long-term financial goals.

REMEMBER: Your ultimate goal is to reorganize your spending so you can live on 70% of your income. You may not be able to hit this target all at once, but the money management resources at **www.youreconomicdestiny.org** can be a big help in saving you time and money. You'll be amazed by how fast you can get out of debt and eliminate the interest payments that are robbing you of your monthly income!

ACTION STEP: ESTABLISH A FAMILY BUDGET TO SET SPENDING PRIORITIES IN LINE WITH YOUR LONG-TERM INVESTMENT STRATEGIES.

If budgeting isn't your favorite activity, I understand. If you're like me, you cringe at the mere mention of the "B" word. That's why I turned to modern technology to help me with this process, and honestly, it worked! I've discovered that this is the best way to keep track of my income and expenses on a consistent basis. It's a fundamental step in applying the principles discussed in this book, such as planning ahead, eliminating debt, saving and investing, and giving to others in need.

However, as I've given financial advice to people from all different income levels, I've repeatedly seen that self-control is not easy for most people. Without an organized plan for budgeting their money, even those who understand basic economic principles will have problems with overspending and properly plugging the holes in their economic basket.

Remember: It's not the *amount* of money you earn that matters; it's how you *manage* what you earn. In order to have a positive economic future, you MUST learn how to live on what you make.

ACTION STEP: MAKE A COMMITMENT TO DESIGN A BUDGET THAT ENABLES YOU TO SPEND WITHIN YOUR MEANS.

You may not be satisfied with your current income. That's fine. In a later chapter, I'll discuss some principles of increase and multiplication that can help you advance in your chosen career.

But don't use your present income as an excuse for poverty or debt. As you're awaiting a promotion or raise, remember these principles:

- Unless you implement a budget, your expenses will always outpace your income.

- If you spend less than you make, you will always have a surplus.

- If you consistently have a surplus from month to month, you eventually will build considerable wealth.

BUDGET FOR YOUR LONG-TERM GOALS

Your budget must set spending priorities, and these priorities must line up with your long-term financial goals. Budgeting helps to take some of the "impulse buying" out of your spending habits, because your spending becomes more focused and targeted toward your true objectives.

Your goal is to manage *every dollar* of your income! You want to begin by avoiding any situation that robs you of your money, and this includes such things as late fees, penalties, interest, fines, traffic tickets, expensive cell phone plans, auto shipment of products you don't really need, auto debits for services you don't use anymore, etc. Always be on the lookout for ways to reduce expenses and cut costs from your monthly budget.

ACTION STEP: CLOSE THE HOLES IN YOUR FINANCIAL BASKET. ELIMINATE ALL UNNECESSARY WASTE, AND REDUCE ALL UNNECESSARY EXPENSES.

REVIEW OF SOME TIPS FOR BEING A GOOD STEWARD

- **SET YOUR SPENDING PRIORITIES.** This should be done in consultation with your family and in accordance with the principles in the Economic Destiny Program. Your goal should be to eventually live on 70% of your income.

- **SET UP AN AUTOMATIC SAVINGS PROGRAM.** After your tithe, you need to "pay yourself first." Your objective should be to accumulate a minimum of three to six months of living expenses in your short-term savings account.

- **PAY CASH FOR EMERGENCIES AND CONSUMER ITEMS.** Keep only one or two credit cards. By saving money on principal and interest payments, you will have more funds available to apply to your debt-elimination program or your wealth-building account.

- **UNDERSTAND THE IMPACT OF YOUR SPENDING HABITS.** Every day, you are faced with spending choices that will ultimately impact your long-term economic destiny. Before spending your money on an item, ask yourself if the purchase will draw you closer to or farther from your financial goals.

  EXAMPLE: John buys one cup of expensive coffee each day. If he took that $4.25 per day and allocated it to his accelerated mortgage reduction plan, he could eliminate 6.5 years of mortgage payments and save $62,492 in interest on his mortgage!

- **USE FINANCIAL MANAGEMENT SOFTWARE.** Software can enable you to see the effects of interest and spending patterns on your long-term goals. This is a fantastic way to have 20/20 financial *foresight* instead of always being the victim of 20/20 financial hindsight.

Now that you've learned the importance of being a good steward of the resources God entrusts to you, you're ready to tackle the next crucial step in the Economic Destiny Program: escaping the bondage of debt.

Chapter 11

FREEDOM FROM BONDAGE
ECONOMIC DESTINY PRINCIPLE #4—
GETTING OUT OF DEBT

"There is no practice more dangerous than that of borrowing money. When money can be had in that way, repayment is seldom thought of in time, the interest becomes a loss, execution to raise [money] by way of industry ceases, it comes easy and is spent freely, and many things are indulged in that would not be thought of if they were to be purchased by the sweat of the brow."
—George Washington

"If you diligently obey the voice of the LORD your God...you shall lend to many nations, but you shall not borrow."
—Deuteronomy 28:1, 12

ONE OF THE MOST IMPORTANT THINGS I've learned about debt and credit is that when we create a debt, we're voluntarily surrendering a part of our future to someone else. Debt is a form of voluntary bondage where the borrower commits to be a servant to the lender until the debt is paid.

Debt is a thief—robbing you of your time, your wealth and your future. Debt causes worry, anxiety and conflicts between family and friends. In addition to destroying your honor and integrity, debt will prevent you from being a blessing to others.

In this chapter, we will examine how you can apply the principles of the Economic Destiny Program to break the power of debt in your life. We will take a close look at the destructive power of debt and the misery it causes most American families. Most important, I will share the practical steps you can take to overcome debt and move toward God's destiny for your life.

In order to understand why debt creates such bondage, we must take a journey back in time to see the roots of debt and how it has been used to shape our history—and how it's still controlling our lives today.

A BRIEF HISTORY OF DEBT AND INTEREST

Before the days of the first recorded contracts and financial transactions, people used cattle, grain, silver bars or anything else they could agree upon as currency to be used in a trade.

Over 3,000 years ago in the city of Uruk (known in the Bible as Erech), people kept tabs of debts (who owed what to whom) on clay tablets. Those tablets contained the earliest known recordings of financial transactions and were discovered in the area known as Mesopotamia.

Many historians who have studied these early contracts and financial records have theorized that this was the very reason writing was originally invented—to keep track of these types of deals. With financial agreements recordable, people began to document what they were owed and what was to be repaid.

At first it was considered inappropriate to receive anything more than the original sum lent. Before long, however, the value of money in relation to time was discovered. Ancient merchants quickly learned that the loss of capital led to the loss of profits. Today, we call this the "time value" of money.

The Sumerians were the first culture known to develop the concept of interest. The Egyptian word for interest is *ms* and means "to give birth." The Sumerian word for interest was *mash*, which was also the word for calves. The concept of returning more or "giving birth" to your asset came from lending cattle.

If you lent someone a herd of 20 cattle for a year, you would expect to be repaid with more than the original 20, because the herd multiplied. The herder's wealth has a natural rate of increase equal to the rate of reproduction of his livestock. Since cattle was the standard currency of the time, loans in all comparable commodities would be expected to "give birth," or grow, as well.

Debt was a powerful motivator in those early times. It became a tool to make people work harder and more efficiently. Crop yields of farmers in debt were significantly higher than those without debt. If farmers could not pay back their loans, they would lose their farm though foreclosure or be forced to sell themselves or their children into slavery. These types of consequences would keep the workers motivated.

While this system of lending may have been great for the wealthy people of Uruk and the rest of the Mesopotamian economy, it made life miserable for working men and women. Some of the first recorded writings by the people in the region of Meso-potamia provide evidence that many people were lamenting their financial situations.

During the reign of Hammurabi from 1792 to 1750 BC, the first regulations of interest, forgiveness of debt, and the extension of credit were developed. Early Hammurabi consumer protection laws were extremely severe. *If you did not pay the borrowed money back as agreed, interest was charged at very high rates.*

Merchants, and sometimes temple owners, made ordinary business loans, charging from 20% for loans on silver bars to 33.3% for loans on grain.

One of Hammurabi's laws for extension of credit stated:

If anyone fails to meet a claim for debt and sells himself, his wife, his son and daughter for money or gives them away to forced labor, they shall work for three years in the house of the man who bought them, or the proprietor, and in the fourth year they shall be set free.

Twelve hundred years after Hammurabi laid down the codes for the first regulations of interest, forgiveness of debt, and extension of credit, the first widely accepted coins were minted, the Athenian silver owls. The use of currency in exchange for labor dates back to 2,500 BC, when silver bars substituted for barley payments. After that, the Mesopotamians used copper coins until silver coins were minted and widely accepted as a method of payment. And thus credit became a useful method of exchange of future labor in lieu of money.

THE HISTORICAL TREATMENT OF DEBTORS

From the very beginning, debt has caused major problems. One of the byproducts of having access to easy credit is the issue of timely repayment. There's a natural tendency to over-pledge our future labor for a term that can't be met.

Laws governing collection of debts and bankruptcy have been in effect for over 400 years to deal with borrowers who cannot make timely repayments of their debts. However, the concept of bankruptcy as we understand it today—"the elimination of debts"—is much different from its original intent.

The word "bankruptcy" comes from the words *bancus*, which means the tradesman's counter, and *ruptus*, which means broken. Thus, it describes one whose place of business is broken or gone.

Some of the first bankruptcy laws originated in Rome under the Caesars. A trustee was appointed to collect the creditor's debts after his or her marketplace bench was broken or removed as a declaration that the merchant had gone bankrupt. The creditor filed the bankruptcy to force the collection of the debts to be paid by the merchant. Although the merchant was unable to immediately discharge the debts owed, he had to make payments until his debts were paid in full.

The first true English bankruptcy law was passed in England in 1570 AD, during the reign of King Henry VIII. This was the foundation of the American bankruptcy laws still used today. But before the first English bankruptcy law was passed, a previous statute on debtors was passed in 1542 AD.

The 1542 statute was designed to prevent frauds on creditors. Under this statute, a creditor could demand that a debtor be summoned to appear before the Chancellor. The debtor was examined under oath, and if he failed to surrender his possessions to pay his debts, he was sent to a debtors' prison.

In 1570 a new bankruptcy statute was passed to solve a growing problem: the debtors' prisons had reached full capacity. Then in 1705, under the English Statute of Anne Bankruptcy Act, uncooperative debtors could be executed. About five people were ultimately executed under this law.

You might think that was too harsh a treatment, but the alternatives were not much better. Early bankruptcy laws had some provisions that would be considered extremely unusual today. For example:

- Only a creditor could commence a bankruptcy case against a debtor, and debtors could not initiate their own bankruptcy.

- Citizens were imprisoned for debts they were unable to pay.

- During a bankruptcy, assets were seized, sold and distributed to creditors, but that did not stop the collection of the remaining monies owed. There was no discharge of the obligation for the remaining debts. Collection efforts continued after the sale of all the debtor's property.

- Bankruptcy commissioners (trustees) could break into a debtor's home and seize any assets they believed could be sold to help satisfy the debt.

- Debtors could have an ear cut off or an ear nailed (while still attached) to a wooden pillory in a public square for everyone to see.

111

YOUR
Economic Destiny

Present-day laws have evolved and are much different from those of our past. We also look at debtors much differently. While debtors are commonly seen as victims today, they originally were looked upon as criminals.

NATIONAL AND PERSONAL DEBT

Of course, debt is a major problem for nations as well as individuals. Ever since the creation of credit, debt and interest, these financial tools have been used to originate, grow, sustain and control national economies and the people in them. Once an individual or a nation commits their future time, talent, skills and resources to a creditor, the creditor will own them, control them, and decide what they'll be doing in the future: working to pay the interest.

With the emergence of highly sophisticated banking and marketing techniques of the 21st century, the craft of luring a person into debt to achieve their dreams, maintain a lifestyle, or develop a sense of security has become widely accepted. There is nothing more powerful and deceptive than the means used by advertisers and credit card companies to lull unwitting people into the bondage of debt.

Today we've been trained not to see debt as the bondage it is. We no longer face the consequences of being thrown into a debtors' prison, nor are we forced to sell our children into slavery to pay off our debts.

But we still trade something for the use of credit and debt— something very costly. When we incur debt, we pay for it with our lives! Debts we created in the past control our freedom today and limit our destiny tomorrow.

Time passes quickly, life happens, and we inevitably feel the need to borrow even *more* money before the previous debt is repaid. Unless we take firm steps to reverse this cycle, it will continue until we've traded our freedom for a lifetime spent in bondage. We may not be in a *literal* debtors' prison—but we're in prison nevertheless.

FREEDOM IS WITHIN YOUR REACH

God says in Deuteronomy 28:12-13 that you can be "the head and not the tail," the lender and not the borrower. This is a direct contradiction of most people's view that it's impossible to live a happy and successful life without debt.

Not only is it *possible* to live the abundant, debt-free life God desires for you to live, but the results are *automatic* to those willing to apply His economic principles to their circumstances. Wealth and financial abundance aren't a matter of luck or "winning life's lottery," but rather they're natural byproducts of following God's eternal, time-tested principles for gaining and preserving wealth.

Debt occurs when an individual, corporation or governmental entity borrows money in order to purchase a product or service, making a commitment to pay back the obligation in the future. Even though a debt normally takes the form of monthly principal and interest payments, it involves something much more serious than that. *Debt is a spirit.* And when it gets out of control, it can render the borrower powerless, because debt has become his master, distracting him from fulfilling his goals and dreams.

There's no great mystery about what causes debt. Rather than being a matter of chance or happenstance, debt usually is accompanied by poor financial stewardship and an improper mindset about money.

KEY PRINCIPLE: BY ITS VERY NATURE, DEBT INVOLVES THE TRANSFER OF WEALTH FROM THE BORROWER TO THE LENDER, FROM ONE PERSON, ORGANIZATION, OR COUNTRY TO ANOTHER. DEBT IS NO RESPECTER OF PERSONS. THOSE WHO DON'T PROPERLY MANAGE DEBT WILL INEVITABLY BECOME IMPOVERISHED BY IT.

In order to get out of debt, you must understand how debt traps and enslaves people. The foundation for how we make our financial decisions is usually established very early in our lives. As a child, we observe how our parents handle money and manage their finances.

Unconsciously, we adopt these same attitudes and habits. They control our lives and form patterns of behavior that are difficult to break.

The mindsets governing our financial decisions have usually been well-established by our early teens. Most of us start off by purchasing our car, clothing and furniture on credit. In many cases, student loans and mortgages are soon added to the debt mix. We haven't even paid off the first item, and we've already found many additional things we feel we need.

Before we know it, we've established a debt habit that will set the tone for the remainder of our lives—unless we take firm and decisive steps to break the pattern. Just like someone hooked on alcohol or drugs, it's very difficult to break this addiction to debt once it's set in motion.

Financial freedom never comes accidently—we must make a decision, a plan, and a commitment to follow through until we've achieved a debt-free lifestyle.

ACTION STEP: REALIZE THAT IT'S POSSIBLE TO LIVE A SUCCESSFUL LIFE WITHOUT DEBT. YOU MUST CHANGE YOUR THINKING BEFORE YOU CAN CHANGE YOUR CIRCUMSTANCES. YOU MUST REPROGRAM YOUR POINT OF VIEW AND CORE BELIEFS REGARDING DEBT.

Too often, those ensnared by debt blame their situation on not making enough money. But once a lifestyle of debt is firmly rooted, the more money a person earns, the more money he or she spends. Without realizing it, they've set a lifelong course of spending more than they earn—a course that will draw them into deeper and deeper financial bondage.

Sadly, few people are sounding an alarm, warning their country-men of the dangers of debt. The principles of personal economics are no longer taught in schools, so how are people going to receive the foundation they need to make sound financial decisions?

WE MUST LOOK TOWARD GOD'S SOUND
FINANCIAL PRINCIPLES!

The Scriptures are very clear about God's perspective on debt, and they provide detailed instructions about how to handle it. In the Old Testament, debt is considered a part of the curse of disobeying God, and He says those who follow His precepts will be lenders rather than borrowers (Deuteronomy 28:12).

So how can we position ourselves to be lenders instead of borrowers? If we follow God's principles regarding stewardship and economic success, we'll automatically accumulate a surplus—the very opposite of incurring debt. This means being able to create short-term and long-term savings and investments. Instead of being stuck on the treadmill of debt, we'll be able to make money as a lender and investor.

This kind of surplus isn't only available to those who make a high income. Even average wage earners can create a surplus if they follow the principles in the Economic Destiny Program. (See the *PRIVATIZED BANKING PLAN (IBC)* discussed in chapter 14.)

However, notice what happens when we do *not* follow God's principles:

> **If you do not obey the voice of the LORD your God, to observe carefully all His commandments and His statutes which I command you today...all these curses will come upon you and overtake you...The alien who is among you shall rise higher and higher above you, and you shall come down lower and lower. He shall lend to you, but you shall not lend to him; he shall be the head, and you shall be the tail (Deuteronomy 28:15, 43-44).**

Deuteronomy 28 illustrates that God has drawn a line in the sand regarding abundance and debt. On the one side, we can experience the blessings He's promised to those who follow His instructions. But on the other side of the line are curses that result from not heeding His principles regarding debt and other issues.

Sadly, many families today are facing the negative consequences of not following God's economic plan. They've become borrowers instead of lenders, the tail instead of the head. Far from being inevitable, these negative outcomes could have been avoided.

Deuteronomy 28 is only one of hundreds of Bible passages that speak of the bondage of debt. Here are a few more:

The borrower becomes the lender's slave (Proverbs 22:7).

You were bought at a price; do not become slaves of men (1 Corinthians 7:23).

Owe no one anything except to love one another (Romans 13:8).

Once we've been programmed to accept borrowing as a standard way to purchase things, this mindset will govern our financial actions in a very predictable way. Since a borrower always becomes the servant of the lender, debt deceptively becomes the master of everyone who trusts it. It cripples people from fulfilling their dreams and weakens the basic foundation of a family's security and prosperity.

God doesn't want our future success hindered by debt or tied to the ups and downs of the world's economy. Instead of being enslaved to our economic circumstances, He wants us to be free to complete our assignment and extend a helping hand to others.

PROPER MOTIVATIONS

Often debt is a byproduct of improper motivations. While our highest motivations in life should be to love God and love people (Mark 12:28-34), our hearts are sometimes drawn away after other interests that have nothing to do with our main purpose for living—and credit is frequently involved in these distractions. We can stop this vicious cycle by beginning to trust that God will be who He said He would be: our Provider.

God has made a promise to you, and HE will not go against His Word once He's made a promise. It's set in stone as sure as the sun will rise tomorrow: He has promised to meet our needs if we follow His principles (Philippians 4:19).

But often we confuse our *needs* with our *wants*. If we feel we "need" a newer car, a bigger house, or more stylish clothes, it's tempting to use debt as our source rather than seeking God's wisdom in the matter.

It's not as difficult as you might think to know when we are violating a financial principle and about to bring ourselves harm rather than blessings. Scripture says: "The blessing of the Lord brings wealth, and he adds no trouble to it" (Proverbs 10:22 NIV).

One of the most often broken financial principles has to do with avoiding surety.

THE TRUTH ABOUT SURETY

What would you do if you lost your job or had an unexpected loss of income that lasted for a long period of time? Would you be able to sustain yourself and your family? Would you be able to maintain your existing lifestyle if there were a serious economic crisis?

Most people manage their lives as if they're living in a perfect world and everything will continue to work predictably as they commit to taking on debt. Surety is a process by which we expose ourselves and future generations not only to the loss of existing resources, but also the loss of everything we've accumulated over time. We should never allow ourselves to get into a surety position—but people do it all the time.

In my financial workshops, people often ask me questions like these:

- "Jeff, isn't there good debt and bad debt?
- "How can I run a business or build wealth on a consistent basis without using some form of debt?"
- "How would I ever be able to purchase a house or car if I couldn't borrow the money?"
- "Are you saying that if I follow God's principles for my finances, it's a sin to ever borrow money?"

117

To such questions, I always respond, "No, it's not a sin to borrow money. Debt is a tool that can be helpful when properly used. But one of the biggest problems with debt is that it often violates the principle of surety."

Of course, many people have never heard of the concept of surety, so it's impossible for them to understand why it's so dangerous. I'm always happy to answer questions like these from students in my workshops, but it takes a little time to explain the principle of surety and how it can have such a negative impact on our lives.

The Bible warns against putting ourselves in a surety position. The dictionary says surety occurs when a person agrees to be legally responsible for the debt, default or conduct of another.

But the Biblical definition of surety is more wide-ranging. It includes making a pledge or commitment to pay a debt without having a sure way (collateral worth more than the debt) to repay it. A person who enters into surety has insufficient collateral to cover the obligation. Most people fall into the trap of expecting to have enough future resources to cover the obligation, but this presumption is unreliable, for the debtor is basing his expectation on circumstances he has no control over.

Usually surety involves pledging or risking what God has already provided as security (collateral) for a future obligation. Even though this principle is warned against throughout the Scriptures, most people don't understand how to apply it to their personal finances or business affairs on a practical level.

When I mention surety, most people automatically think of cosigning for someone else's loan. Although this is certainly a *form* of surety, it only scratches the surface of what the principle includes. Unwittingly, many people are suffering the consequences of violating this settled principle in God's Word. Again we see that "people are destroyed for lack of knowledge" (Hosea 4:6).

Solomon, the richest man who ever lived, had a lot to say about surety:

> Do not be one of those who shakes hands in a pledge, one of those who is surety for debts (Proverbs 22:26).

> A man devoid of understanding shakes hands in a pledge, and becomes surety for his friend (Proverbs 17:18).

My son, if you become surety for your friend, if you have shaken hands in pledge for a stranger, you are snared by the words of your mouth; you are taken by the words of your mouth. So do this, my son, and deliver yourself; for you have come into the hand of your friend: Go and humble yourself; plead with your friend. Give no sleep to your eyes, nor slumber to your eyelids. Deliver yourself like a gazelle from the hand of the hunter, and like a bird from the hand of the fowler (Proverbs 6:1-5).

Solomon's conclusion is clear: Surety is a deceptive trap, and we must avoid it at all costs!

AVOIDING SURETY

Surety is an instrument used as security against loss, damage or failure to perform as agreed. It can be created when you guarantee debt either for yourself or for someone else.

You avoid surety by always having sufficient cash or collateral to cover the value of the purchase.

An example of surety is when you go into debt to purchase a car (the collateral), and it ends up being worth less than what you owe on the loan. For example, if you buy a car for $20,000 with no down payment, the value of the car immediately drops when you drive it off the lot. If the car is only worth $16,000, but the debt owed is $20,000, you are in a surety position for $4,000. If for some reason you can't meet the monthly payment and the car is repossessed or you have to sell it at the present market value, you will still owe the balance of $4,000, since your collateral is worth less than the debt.

The same principle holds true for real estate transactions. Suppose you bought a home appraised at $400,000, but because of a drop in the real estate market, the house is now only worth $325,000. You are "under water" in the amount of $75,000.

In order to avoid surety, you must carefully examine the economic realities of your home, car or business assets prior to making a purchase that involves debt. Otherwise, you are likely to end up in a surety position.

Sadly, many families don't realize they're in a surety position until it's too late. For example, the real estate market has generally been increasing in value over the past 40 years, and you could always sell your home for more than what you paid. In recent years, however, most real estate prices have decreased, and many people have found themselves in a home that is worth less than the balance they owe on their mortgage. They are in a surety position.

The best way to avoid surety in residential real estate is to make a sufficient down payment. Since buying a home will be one of the most important decisions you will ever make, you should follow the instructions on how to purchase a home and build equity into it quickly. This is outlined in the next chapter, "Transforming Waste to Wealth."

ACTION STEP: SET A GOAL TO OWN YOUR HOME FREE AND CLEAR. USING THE BUILT-IN TOOLS OF THE ECONOMIC DESTINY PROGRAM, YOU CAN REDUCE YOUR MORTGAGE QUICKLY SO YOU ARE NO LONGER IN A POSITION OF SURETY.

WHEN LIABILITIES ARE GREATER THAN ASSETS

Another category of surety is when a person's liabilities are greater than their assets. This means the market value of what they own is less than their total debt. In the finance industry this is called a negative net worth, and it's usually the result of spending more than they make on monthly basis.

If someone is earning $3,000 per month but is consistently spending $3,100 per month, he or she is already in a surety position—pledging future income to pay for current expenditures. Because of the ease of credit card purchases, the average family does not keep proper records of what they spend. In most case they're not even aware that they're spending more money than they earn. Credit card debt usually accumulates over a period of time and ultimately causes serious financial problems.

If this describes *your* situation, your total financial position is out of balance. In essence, you are already insolvent, even though you may be earning a substantial income. If you were to liquidate your assets, you would not have a sure way to pay the balance of your debt. This means you have to count on future earnings to pay your present obligations.

Whether you realize it or not, this is a position of surety—and you're living in bondage. If you're in this position, get out of it as fast as you can!

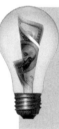 **ACTION STEPS:** AVOID USING YOUR HOME AS EQUITY TO CONSOLIDATE OTHER DEBT. ALSO, STAY AWAY FROM REVERSE MORTGAGES AND OTHER PROGRAMS THAT WOULD CAUSE YOU TO RE-MORTGAGE YOUR HOME ONCE IT IS PAID FOR.

ELIMINATING CREDIT CARD BONDAGE

By far the most destructive form of surety today is the improper use of credit cards. When you make a purchase on a credit card and don't have enough money in savings to cover the bill, you are making a pledge to pay out of your future resources—without any certainty that the money will be there. In other words, there is no collateral in place to secure the debt. This means that every dollar applied on your credit card is surety by definition.

REMEMBER: When you use credit cards, you are extremely vulnerable to surety and the multiplication of debt.

ACTION STEP: THE ONLY WAY TO AVOID SURETY WITH CREDIT CARDS IS TO MAKE A COMMITMENT TO PAY YOUR CREDIT CARD DEBT IN FULL AT THE END OF EACH MONTH. IF YOU DON'T HAVE THE MONEY TO PAY YOUR CREDIT CARD IN FULL AT THE END OF THE MONTH, YOU SHOULD NOT USE THE CARD, BECAUSE TO DO SO WOULD MEAN BREAKING GOD'S SURETY PRINCIPLE.

Under the Economic Destiny Program, you will be creating a short-term savings account, which you pay into every month. If you run into an emergency and need immediate cash, you can simply borrow the money from yourself—using your short-term savings instead of going into debt. Then you can pay yourself back the money you took from savings. We recommend that you pay yourself back "with interest" just like you would pay back the bank.

WHAT ABOUT BUSINESS DEBT?

Many business people take calculated risks to invest a portion of their income in hopes of receiving a future return on their money. Of course, a certain amount of risk is involved in *any* business or *any* type of business investments.

While there is nothing wrong with prudent business investments, some people go far beyond this. Adopting a get-rich-quick "lottery" mentality, they bet their entire future on "one roll of the dice"—a major business deal that will either bankrupt them or make them rich for life.

In essence, such people are going into surety, using resources they've already accumulated as collateral to borrow on their future. But what happens if a major project should fail? If the business person is overly leveraged, he risks losing both the assets he's accumulated and his ongoing business, not to mention his good name.

After losing his savings, destroying his credit rating, and disrupting the lives of his employees, such a person would have to start over.

As good stewards, we should never put ourselves in a surety position. As tempting as it may seem at times, we should never risk our entire business or savings on any one project. As Luke 14:28 instructs us, we should examine the outcome and count the cost before a major commitment is made.

ACTION STEP: NEVER MAKE A COMMITMENT OF YOUR TIME OR RESOURCES WITHOUT CONSIDERING THE LONG-TERM CONSEQUENCES.

Even in the best of times, we should never "put all our eggs in one basket." We must count the cost to ensure that if our venture fails, we will still have enough left over to keep from exposing our business to complete ruin.

ORGANIZING YOUR DEBT-ELIMINATION PROGRAM

No matter what your background or economic status may be, the principles outlined in this book will work for you. *Anyone* who applies them to their lives will reap the benefits. By following these simple steps, you can be completely debt-free (including your home) without substantially changing your existing lifestyle. Once the process is set into motion, its success is certain, for these time-tested principles have produced long-term financial success for countless people over the centuries.

REMEMBER: Every dollar you spend on interest payments is money taken directly from your disposable income. Your goal is to live debt-free or have a maximum debt of 10% of your annual income. Ideally, you should pay off all credit card debts at the end of the month in which the purchase is made. That way you can avoid interest payments altogether.

THE ONLY WAY TO BREAK THE HABIT OF DEBT IS TO STOP ANY ADDITIONAL CREDIT PURCHASES UNTIL YOU ARE DEBT-FREE, AND THIS ESPECIALLY APPLIES TO CREDIT CARD DEBT.

Once you are out of debt, you must avoid putting yourself in a surety position ever again. This will take some discipline and guidance, but you can do it—particularly with the help of the resources available at our website.

Since principal and interest payments are the largest expense item for the average family, most families will automatically increase their disposable income by as much as one-third if they're able to eliminate these payments. The money saved can then be applied to their surplus account.

Consider this: Every dollar you spend on interest payments is gone forever! It could have been working for you if it had been placed in an interest-bearing account. While a dollar spent on interest is gone, a dollar invested properly will produce many more dollars.

ACTION STEP: BEGIN A DEBT-REDUCTION PLAN WITH A GOAL TO LIVE DEBT-FREE WITHIN THREE TO FIVE YEARS. ALTHOUGH IT'S NOT ALWAYS WRONG TO PURCHASE ITEMS ON CREDIT, YOU MUST REMEMBER THAT YOUR ULTIMATE OBJECTIVE IS TO HAVE NO CAR PAYMENTS AND NO MORTGAGE PAYMENTS UNLESS YOU ARE SELF-FINANCING THEM FROM YOUR OWN BANKING SYSTEM (DISCUSSED IN CHAPTER 14). THIS WILL PUT YOU IN AN ELITE GROUP OF PEOPLE WHO ARE ALREADY EXPERIENCING FINANCIAL FREEDOM.

GETTING STARTED ON YOUR DEBT-ELIMINATION PROGRAM

The Economic Destiny Program is designed to assist you in eliminating all debt, using only your current income. By eliminating debt, you can increase the amount of income you keep by almost 35% (see the following charts). Notice that you are able to give, save, and even improve your lifestyle.

Before and After Implementing the Economic Destiny Debt-Elimination Program

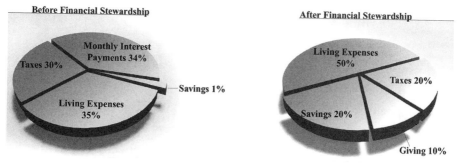

Before Financial Stewardship

After Financial Stewardship

REMEMBER: The Economic Destiny Program is much different from your normal get-out-of-debt diets that just have you buying more books and attending more seminars. From the very first day, you will be taking purposeful interest cancelation actions which will add up to thousands of dollars in interest savings. You will be able to begin this process without a major lifestyle change and you will have all the support you need to eliminate your debts, you just need to make the commitment to begin.

ACTION STEP: TO BE SUCCESSFUL, YOU MUST HAVE AN EMOTIONAL ENGAGEMENT IN THE PROCESS. YOU MUST BECOME SO FED UP WITH YOUR EXISTING CIRCUMSTANCES THAT YOU MAKE A COMMITMENT NOT TO TOLERATE DEBT ANY LONGER. MAKE YOUR DECLARATION OUT LOUD, AND MARK THE DATE ON YOUR CALENDAR! IF YOU FOLLOW THROUGH, YOUR FINANCIAL INDEPENDENCE WILL BE JUST A FEW YEARS AWAY.

TOOLS FOR ACCELERATING YOUR DEBT-REDUCTION PLAN

If you're serious about accelerating your debt-reduction plan, we suggest that you utilize the Economic Destiny Debt-Elimination Software, because it's a simple and powerful tool for implementing the principles discussed in the Economic Destiny Program.

In addition to supercharging your debt-elimination program, this software will enable you to:

1. Put your debt-elimination and wealth-building program on autopilot.

2. Learn financial literacy principles while eliminating debt.

3. Consistently track your progress.

4. Benefit from a built-in mentorship and accountability program.

5. Will show you the fastest ways to zero debt while paying the least amount of interest on your debts during the pay-down process.

6. See the consequences of your financial choices *before* you make them, so you can determine the best course of action without having to pay an advisor every time you need solid planning advice.

For many people, this software is the difference between *real* financial peace and never-ending financial frustration. It provides the added discipline most of us need for keeping on track. Instead of being merely a get-out-of-debt diet, this is a tool that helps you implement a dynamic plan that fits within your current lifestyle.

Think about it: You can have a built-in Economic Destiny Coach in the comfort of your own home, helping you make wise financial decisions that will make a huge impact on your ability to hit your goals. It's like putting your finances on autopilot!

By properly managing 100% of each dollar, you'll be able to reach financial goals you never thought possible. As you dramatically reduce your interest costs, you can redirect your money toward building a surplus for you and your family in line with the principles of the Economic Destiny Program (see www.youreconomicdestiny.org for more information).

CONCLUSIONS

In this chapter, we've discussed how to escape from the trap of debt and surety. We illustrated how your disposable income can dramatically increase when you eliminate interest payments.

Although it's OK to purchase certain items on credit, remember that your ultimate objective is to never pay interest to anyone other than yourself. That means paying off any debts as soon as possible, so your income can be funneled toward savings and investments rather than interest payments. Soon you can be *earning* interest rather than *paying* interest.

People who enjoy financial security have learned how to save and earn interest rather than go into debt and pay interest. They're experiencing the joy of putting their money to work for them rather than constantly handing over their money to lenders.

In the next chapter, you'll learn how to build wealth by eliminating waste. You'll discover how to unlock the maximum potential from the resources you already have. We still have some ground to cover in order for you to reach your full economic potential and walk in the economic freedom you desire. So keep reading and watch the transformation begin! Knowledge can change your life— when you apply it. Let's move on and learn how to transform waste into wealth.

Chapter 12
TRANSFORMING WASTE TO WEALTH
ECONOMIC DESTINY PRINCIPLE #5— ELIMINATE WASTE

"Waste is worse than loss. The time is coming when every person who lays claim to ability will keep the question of waste before him constantly. The scope of thrift is limitless.
—Thomas Edison

"There was a rich man whose manager was accused of wasting his possessions. So he called him in and asked him, 'What is this I hear about you? Give an account of your management, because you cannot be manager any longer."
—Luke 16:1-2 NIV

WE'VE DISCUSSED THE IMPORTANCE of planning ahead and establishing a surplus to build long-term wealth, but many people are spending more money than they have coming in. Often the problem is that we've been conditioned to believe there are numerous things we simply *must* have to survive. Seduced by slick advertising and crippled by a short-term view of reality, it's no wonder people struggle to build long-term wealth.

Why are so few Americans able to save money and build a surplus? Often we've been lured by easy credit and deceptive financial products into wasting our resources. As a result, we purchase things we don't really need, paying far too much in the process. We've never been taught how to strategically use our resources to cancel debt and interest payments. This limits our ability to achieve our financial objectives.

The good news is that by making some simple adjustments in our personal economies, much of this waste can be avoided. By following the principles outlined in the Economic Destiny Program, we can close the holes in our financial baskets and accumulate enough surplus to not only meet our own needs, but also to have enough left over to impact the lives of others.

You need practical advice on how to make wise decisions and eliminate waste—and that's exactly what you're going to learn in this chapter. By strategically eliminating waste, you will have a significant rise in your disposable income.

KEYS TO TURNING WASTE INTO WEALTH

In order to build sustainable wealth, you must get the maximum benefit from your income.

In this chapter, we'll examine ways you can get the maximum mileage from your money. One of the best ways to do this is by eliminating waste from the major items in your budget—home, automobile, insurance and taxes. We'll also look at how you can redirect these funds to build long-term wealth.

ACTION STEP: MAXIMIZE YOUR DEBT-REDUCTION PROGRAM BY IDENTIFYING FUNDS YOU DIDN'T REALIZE YOU HAD. REMEMBER: YOU—NOT YOUR CIRCUMSTANCES—SHOULD DICTATE WHERE YOUR MONEY GOES.

In this chapter, I will share specific steps you can take now to maximize your income and minimize waste. You will learn how to:

- Own your home in 7 to 10 years or less—and save 50% to 70% on mortgage payments using just your current income.
- Save up to 50% when purchasing a car.
- Turn liabilities into assets by applying the *"IBC."*
- Save money on taxes.

PURCHASE ASSETS INSTEAD OF LIABILITIES

God's economic plan is built upon sound wisdom and proven success:

Through wisdom a house is built, and by understanding it is established;

By knowledge the rooms are filled with all precious and pleasant riches (Proverbs 24:3-4).

The average American family spends its income on things that *decrease* in value, such as cars, clothes and entertainment. However, the Economic Destiny Program enables you to make choices that facilitate long-term wealth and turn depreciating liabilities into appreciating assets. The ultimate goal is to be able to give more to those in need and leave a financial legacy for your family.

One step in this process involves where you live. Instead of stacking up rent receipts, I recommend that you purchase your home and start building equity.

 **ACTION STEP:** INVEST IN ASSETS THAT INCREASE IN VALUE INSTEAD OF LIABILITIES THAT DECREASE IN VALUE. OBJECTIVE: OWN YOUR HOUSE AND CARS FREE AND CLEAR.

OWNING YOUR HOME FREE AND CLEAR IN 7 TO 10 YEARS...OR LESS!

Owning your home free and clear will facilitate rapid growth of wealth beyond what you've ever imagined. Your home will normally be your most valuable asset and also your most significant liability/

expenditure. This makes it extremely important to get the maximum return for your home dollars.

There are two primary areas to consider when eliminating waste regarding your home: the purchase price and the interest you pay over the life of your mortgage. If you understand how to do this, you will prosper.

A home mortgage is one of the largest transfers of the American family's wealth. Home mortgages are an extremely profitable business, and over the past 60 years the federal government has become involved in the lion's share of mortgages in this country.

In a recently published report, it was estimated that the government controls over 95% of all mortgages in America. Why is this important to you? Because most people think that because they hold the keys to the front door, they are homeowners. This is not true, and it's easy to prove—just miss a few mortgage payments and see who comes asking for *their* keys!

When I speak of your economic freedom under the Economic Destiny Program, I'm referring to genuine "*home* ownership," not "*loan* ownership." The entire concept of property ownership is under attack by the government and the banking industry. No wonder people are confused about what home ownership really means, thinking that **loan** ownership is equivalent to **home** ownership.

Both the government and the banks have taught us that as long as the loan has a competitive interest rate and low monthly payment, we're fulfilling the American dream by "owning" a home. But here's the problem under this approach:

INSTEAD OF YOU TRULY OWNING THE HOME, THE HOME MORTGAGE ENDS UP OWNING YOU!

Most Americans now accept highly mortgaged homes as the norm—but this isn't the norm under the Economic Destiny Program.

I went into the mortgage business to help families, because I believed that mortgages were a necessary tool, a means to an end. But what I soon discovered was something completely different—that mortgages in America are purposely structured to never end.

In the last chapter, you learned that your entire financial destiny is impacted by the interest you pay on your debts. The longer a lender can keep you paying interest, the further away you are from earning interest income and building wealth. You also learned that every dollar committed to past debts is a seed you're unable to plant for your future harvest. Your income is being placed in a bag with holes, where it's quickly lost.

ACTION STEP: SAVE 50% TO 70% WHEN FINANCING A HOME.

If you are going to manage every dollar to get the maximum return, you must invest your resources wisely and look for ways to plug the holes in your economic bucket.

Listed below are a number of proven ways to begin saving hundreds of thousands of dollars when purchasing a new home and managing your mortgage. Regardless of whether you have an existing mortgage or are in the process of obtaining a new mortgage, keep in mind that your ultimate goal is to own your home free and clear, with zero monthly payments. And you want to do this as soon as possible!

Using the tools described in the Economic Destiny Program, you can accomplish the goal of owning your home free and clear in 7 to 10 years or less without refinancing. If that sounds like an impossible dream, I assure you it's not.

GETTING THE BIGGEST BANG FOR YOUR HOMEOWNER DOLLARS

When financing your new home: I recommend obtaining a 30-year fixed mortgage and then using the options listed to reduce the term and overall interest payments. The 30-year fixed mortgage is the best choice, because it gives you more flexibility if you run into a tight financial situation. A 30-year fixed mortgage payment is consistent and predictable, in contrast with unpredictable financial seasons, market cycles, and income levels. Because you're entering into a 30-year mortgage (long-term debt), do not do this with short-term thinking (seeking "a monthly payment you can afford"). Instead of following the terms set by the bank and making payments for the full 30 years, you're going to pay off your 30-mortgage in 7 to 10 years or less, using the tools and resources outlined in the Economic Destiny Program.

Refinancing your home: For many years, the rule of thumb has been to refinance your home if the market interest rate is two points lower than the rate you are currently paying. Take heed: A critical piece of financial literacy has been left out of this equation.

If you're refinancing a mortgage, you may have already spent several years paying on the 30-year term. During the first 5 to 7 years of the loan, you paid mostly interest. You don't want to start paying those front-end-loaded interest payments all over again. Instead, request a term of 15, 20 or 25 years and then use the Economic Destiny debt-elimination strategy to pay off your mortgage as soon as possible. By doing this, you will save tens of thousands of dollars in interest, and you may still be able to lower your monthly payment.

This monthly savings can be strategically applied to your principal in order to accelerate your mortgage payoff, or the difference can be used to fund your *Privatized Banking Plan (IBC)*. Unless you are wise and proactive on this, refinancing will just prolong your payoff and create more debt.

MANAGING YOUR MORTGAGE PAYOFF

If you have mortgage loans I highly recommend using a mortgage accelerator program. I can't stress enough how long-term principal and interest payments will prohibit you from building wealth and reaching your financial goals. The right program will enable you to have a 30-year, 20-year, or 15-year mortgage paid off in only 7 to 10 years or less, using only the income you are currently making. You can save hundreds of thousands of dollars in interest without having to refinance or consolidate your debt.

UNDERSTANDING MORTGAGE ACCELERATION

Mortgage acceleration has been around for more than 16 years in several other countries, and it's even offered by the banks in those countries as a way to eliminate a 30-year mortgage more quickly. Countless families have reaped its amazing benefits.

Mortgage acceleration uses four key banking principles, which have largely been hidden from the average consumer until this past decade. For many years, the banks have used these powerful tools to quickly eliminate their interest payments, increase their assets, and reduce their liabilities. The Economic Destiny Program enables you to do what the banks do and put these same tools to work for *you*.

Mortgage and debt acceleration is not as simple as making extra payments. If it were that easy, I would simply advise you to *make extra payments!* Don't misunderstand me, making extra monthly payments *will* help you pay off your mortgage and other debts sooner. But to maximize the efficiency of every dollar you earn, I recommend using the latest acceleration software tools to put your current income to work in the right amounts, at the right times, and in the right places. The right mortgage accelerator software will *not* require you to take out a new home equity loan, for you don't want to go into even *more* debt in order to get *out* of debt.

Debt acceleration uses four key banking principles:

KEY #1: INTEREST CANCELATION
KEY #2: INTEREST FLOAT
KEY #3: INTEREST ACCUMULATION

KEY #4: STRATEGIC PAYOFF

Figure 6.0 compares four different plans to pay off a $200,000, 30-year mortgage, at a 6.0% interest rate, and with a required monthly payment of $1,199.10:

1. A normal 30-year loan program
2. A biweekly mortgage payment program

3. A normal 30-year loan but paying $200 extra to principal every month

4. A 30-year loan on a mortgage accelerator program

FIGURE **6.0**

Mortgage Plan	Monthly Payment	Months to pay off	Principal paid	Total interest paid
Regular 30-year plan	$1,199.10	360	$200,000	$237,677.00
Using biweekly payments	$1,199.10	294	$200,000	$180,722.00
30-year plan & $200 extra	$1,199.10 + $200	251	$200,000	$151,876.00
Accelerator plan	$1,199.10	113	$200,000	$72,354.00

Conclusion: According to Figure 6.0, with a mortgage accelerator plan, you can pay off the same mortgage in 9.42 years or less, saving $165,323 in interest. You're still going to pay the entire principal amount, but without making extra payments every month. If you tried to match the results of using the accelerator software, you would have to send an estimated $2,410 along with your normal mortgage payment every month, without missing one month for 9.42 years! That's *three times* your current monthly payment!

If you can make outrageous payments like that, then get started today! But if you can't, then these software tools were made for you. The interest savings is very significant, but that's only half the picture. Look at what it's costing you to *not* use these powerful tools to put a quick end to the huge negative wealth transfer your mortgage is costing you.

Figure 7.0 shows the wealth you could have built if you eliminated the $1,199.10 mortgage payment in 9.42 years and reinvested that monthly payment for the remaining 20.58 years of the 30-year mortgage term.

Figure 7.0

Monthly contribution	Interest rate	Years	Nest Egg
$1,199.10	0%	20.58	$296,129.74
$1,199.10	4%	20.58	$472,373.00
$1,199.10	6%	20.58	$602,996.00

It's imperative for you to see how much your monthly mortgage payment is *really* costing you. The longer you pay on your mortgage, the longer you will stay on the wrong side of interest! Each day you're not managing your mortgage pay-off with the proper financial tools, you're transferring more of your financial resources to someone else—which is keeping you from reaching your goals.

THE MIRACLE OF COMPOUND INTEREST

"The most fascinating invention I have ever seen is 'compound interest.' Those who understand it will earn it, and those who don't will pay it." —Albert Einstein

For most people, it's quite a paradigm shift to realize they can eliminate their mortgage in half or one-third the time. We've been trained to transfer much more of our financial resources to someone else than we really need to, thus allowing someone else to control our financial future. You might be saying to yourself, "Jeff, if what you are telling me is true, then how come I've never seen this as a possibility before?"

Take a close look at **Figure 8.0**:

Figure 8.0

Figure 8.0 is a logo you've probably seen thousands of times. But notice that it's possible to view something from several different perspectives. Although you may have seen this logo on a nearly daily basis, have you really seen the entire picture?

Perhaps you've never noticed the arrow pointing to the right. Look between the E and the x. Do you see it now?

Here's the point of this illustration: Often we need someone else to point out what has been right in front of our eyes.

DEBUNKING A COMMON MYTH

Many people have swallowed a common myth about owning their home free and clear:

"I DON'T WANT TO PAY OFF MY MORTGAGE, BECAUSE I WOULD LOSE MY TAX DEDUCTION!"

Think about how ludicrous this reasoning is. You should *never* go into debt to receive a tax deduction! Paying mortgage interest is a waste of your resources, and the waste is *never* offset by your tax savings. Paying interest prevents you from building wealth and limits your ability to create a large surplus account. It ultimately prevents you from leaving a significant financial legacy for the next generation.

So where did this deduction myth come from? One day your tax advisor or loan officer told you something like this: "Now that you're making more money, you need some tax deductions. So it's time to buy a house, for the interest on the mortgage is tax deductable."

Consider *why* they told you this: *It's their job!* The loan officer's job is to sell more loans on behalf of the bank. And your tax advisor may be skilled at helping you minimize taxes, but they're probably NOT skilled at helping you build long-term wealth!

Let's look at the numbers just to make sure you've got the lesson:

- If your gross annual income is $70,000, and you're paying $14,000 a year in mortgage interest to the banker, your new taxable income becomes $56,000.

- Your tax savings for doing this is approximately $3,800. So what happened? You traded $14,000 for $3,800!

- If your mortgage was paid off, you could have paid the IRS the $3,800 in taxes and kept the $10,200 difference.

- And if you *really* needed the tax deduction, you could have donated $14,000 to your church or charity and received your $3,800 tax break for making a significant difference in the lives of others!

If you're still convinced that paying mortgage interest is a good tax write-off, then how come you would spend an entire month shopping for the lowest interest rate on your home loan? The higher your interest rate is, the larger the write-off you would get! But as you can see, the numbers just don't add up in your favor.

ACTION STEP: SAVE 25% TO 40% WHEN PURCHASING A HOME.

SAVING MONEY ON YOUR HOME PURCHASE

Did you know you might be able to buy a house wholesale? This often is possible at courthouse auctions, VA or FHA repossessions, or directly from the bank's repossession inventory. You can locate these purchases through your local newspaper, a real estate agent, the Internet, or various federal agencies operating in your local housing market.

Foreclosed houses are everywhere these days. Check with your County Courthouse or local banks for their auctions on foreclosed homes.

By paying wholesale, you may be able to save as much as 25% to 40% off the retail cost of the home. Your objective is to buy a house below market value, which enables you to have instant equity.

In addition to looking for houses being sold at wholesale prices, there's another strategy you may want to consider. Many people purchase an older home to fix up and live in for two or three years. Then they sell the house and use the profit for their next home. By leaving the equity in their home and trading up, they soon are able to truly *own* their home.

Before signing a contract to purchase a home or obligate yourself to a mortgage, consult with your financial coach or a real estate attorney.

ACTION STEP: TAKE THE MONEY YOU SAVED ON PRINCIPAL AND INTEREST PAYMENTS AND HAVE IT AUTOMATICALLY DEPOSITED INTO YOUR LONG-TERM WEALTH-BUILDING ACCOUNT TO DEVELOP YOUR RETIREMENT NEST EGG.

PURCHASING YOUR NEXT CAR

For the average American family, their cars will be their most expensive purchases other than their houses. **REMEMBER:** Under the Economic Destiny Program, your objective is to be free from any car payments. If you are currently financing your car, set a goal to pay it off early.

Keep in mind that the best way to purchase a vehicle is to borrow from your cash reserves and pay yourself back with principal and interest via the *PRIVATIZED BANKING SYSTEM "IBC,"* discussed in chapter 14. If you are borrowing the bank's money to purchase your vehicles, you are putting yourself in a position of servitude. Your money is working hard for someone else instead of for you. It's that simple!

If you currently pay cash for your cars, you are much better off than if you finance them. But even then, you're still not maximizing your automotive dollars as much as you could. While paying cash is a better option than going into debt, there's an even *better* solution than believing the "cash is king" mantra!

It's important that you learn the "time value" of money and what "opportunity costs" really mean to your financial future. Americans usually spend more money on cars to get them *to work* than they'll ever save in their retirement accounts *at work*. Crazy isn't it?

One inherent problem with car purchases is that you are buying something that will rapidly decrease in value. In contrast, you want to devote as much of your money as possible to purchasing assets that *increase* in value. That is one of the main keys to building long-term wealth.

But you need a car, right? The Economic Destiny Program has it covered. But it also includes a financial strategy to put a permanent end to financing your cars through banks. I'm going to teach you a core banking principle that will turn this depreciating liability into an appreciating asset.

ACTION STEP: SAVE UP TO 50% ON THE PURCHASE OF A CAR BY BUYING ONE THAT IS TWO OR THREE YEARS OLD.

Example: A new car depreciates as soon as you drive it off the lot, and the most rapid depreciation period is within the first two or three years. Knowing this, let someone else pay for this rapid depreciation, and then purchase the car when it's three years old.

At this point, you may be asking, "But Jeff, what if the dealer is offering 1.9% or 0.0% financing on a brand-new car. That's cheap money, right? At face value it may seem that way, but let's look at the bigger picture.

If you purchase a $25,000 car at 0.0% interest and that car's value after four years is only $15,000, then the car really cost you $10,000 over four years. This is a 40% loss over four years, or 10% each year. Even though you paid 0.0% in interest under this scenario, you still lost money on your "investment." The 0% interest enticement was already built into the price of the car. The finance company didn't lose any money on that 0% deal, and they never do.

You see, you really finance *everything* you buy. You're either paying interest to someone else, or you're giving up interest you could have earned if your money was invested in something that increased in value. In the example above, you lost 40% of the car's value, and it didn't really matter whether you lost your money to interest or to deprecation—it was still a losing proposition. So don't be fooled by low interest rate offers on depreciating items.

SO HOW CAN YOU BE A WISE STEWARD OVER EVERY DOLLAR THAT'S ENTRUSTED TO YOUR CARE, WHEN IT'S OBVIOUS THAT 99% OF ALL CARS DEPRECIATE IN VALUE?

The answer is, you can learn to BECOME YOUR OWN BANKER™. Your money needs to be earning interest, multiplying and compounding at all times. When your cash is locked up in a car, it's no longer earning interest dollars for you.

This loss of value and interest is called "opportunity cost," meaning you've lost the opportunity to have your cash compounding and multiplying at all times. The *IBC* strategy described in chapter 14 enables you to reverse the flow of your money and recapture every dollar spent on all your major purchases. Best of all, you can recapture interest income that normally would have been lost.

By reversing the flow of your money, your next car can already be paid for by the time you're ready to purchase the next one.

SAVE ON INCOME TAXES TOO

Saving on taxes can play a major role in helping you reach your Economic Destiny goals. Over your lifetime, you can save hundreds of thousands of dollars in unnecessary taxes, and this will assist you in leaving an abundant financial legacy to your children, grandchildren or charitable interests. I will cover this in detail in the next chapter, "Becoming a Wise Investor."

A QUICK REVIEW

In this chapter, we discussed the importance of eliminating waste from your current expenditures. With the money you save, you can reduce debt and fund your short-term emergency savings account and your long-term wealth-building account.

Many of us are unwittingly caught in the trap of wasting financial resources. We are buying things on impulse or buying things we don't really need. We often pay too much for our homes, cars, insurance premiums, and taxes, and we're wasting our resources on excessive interest payments.

By eliminating waste, you can reduce your current spending and begin to establish a surplus. With a few simple changes, you can build a multimillion dollar retirement fund that will bless your family and leave a legacy for future generations.

At **www.youreconomicdestiny.org** I've assembled some powerful money-saving tips. It's my sincere desire to help you eliminate waste and discover a "lifestyle of thrift," so you can build your surplus quickly. By utilizing the cost-saving tips on the website, you can save from 50% to 75% on many kinds of services you are currently paying too much for.

Now that you are learning how to reduce waste to build wealth, it's time to become a wise investor and begin multiplying your resources.

Chapter 13 ——————————————

BECOMING A WISE INVESTOR
ECONOMIC DESTINY PRINCIPLE #6—
CHANGING SURPLUS INTO ABUNDANCE

*"Steady plodding brings prosperity, hasty speculation
brings poverty"* —*Proverbs 21:5 TLB*

*"He who has a slack hand becomes poor, but the
hand of the diligent makes rich"* —*Proverbs 10:4*

I RECENTLY RECEIVED A CALL from a woman named "Nancy." She just turned 58 and was distraught that during the past few years she and her husband "Ted" had taken $100,000 from their retirement account to invest as down payments to build two homes. They were going to live in one of the homes and then sell the other to pay off half of their new residence. They figured that this would enable them to retire with a low monthly payment.

Unfortunately, things didn't go as they planned. The values of both homes have fallen by 25%, so instead of selling the second home at a loss, they decided to rent it out until home values move up again. Nancy told me they are paying $780 per month to make up the difference between the mortgage payment and the rent they receive.

To make matters worse, they've had to borrow from their 401(k) to cover the $780 shortfall every month. Nancy went on to say with a frustrated, shaky tone, "If we sell the homes now, we will only be able to recover $25,000 of our original $100,000 investment, and if we don't sell in the next 24 months, we will drain our entire 401(k) just to keep up with this treadmill were on."

At that point, I asked Nancy if their entire savings was invested in the 401(k). Nancy said yes and went on to explain that they'd been investing a significant portion of each paycheck in their 401(k) plans. This originally seemed like a great idea because of the tax breaks, but Nancy described the very sad outcome of this choice: "We lost 40% of our 401(k) value in the market crash last year. We had planned on taking yearly distributions of about $45,000 starting next year, but that estimate has shrunk to a little under $19,000."

The more I enquired about Nancy and Ted's situation, the worse the scenario seemed. "According to the administrator of Ted's 401(k), it's likely to take 17 years for our account to regain its value," Nancy lamented. "We will be nearly 80 before the loss is recovered. And that's *if* the market doesn't have another downturn and *if* we forego taking an annual distributions until we're 72! But we don't really have a choice—we will have to start taking that distribution next year just to cover our rent and food."

Before I could respond, she added something that completely shocked me. With a touch of anger in her voice, Nancy said, "The 401(k) administrator and our financial planner had told us not to worry about deferring the taxes until after age 59½, since we would probably be in a lower tax bracket by then. He didn't know how right he would be. On the verge of hitting 59½, we are statistically broke!"

I could feel her pain as she continued, "We are so tired of the roller coaster ride. We have worked hard over the years to position ourselves for a good retirement, but now we're witnessing all our efforts going down the drain."

On the verge of tears, Nancy concluded her sad story, "It makes us sick to see years of investments and mortgage payments become worthless. We thought we would have something to pass on to our children, but there will be nothing left. And we can't see anything we can do to correct this situation—there's just not enough time left for us."

Although I didn't agree with Nancy's perspective that all hope was gone, I certainly could empathize with her pain and frustration.

IS THERE HOPE FOR NANCY AND TED?

Unfortunately, the options for Nancy and Ted are more limited now, because time is no longer on their side. And the coming economic storms could make their recovery even more difficult. But if they're willing to take action now to follow sound economic principles and leverage the tools and strategies of a wise investor, they can still achieve financial independence and leave a legacy for their children.

At the close of my conversation with Nancy, I assured her, "I know for a fact that all hope is not lost. There still are options you and Ted can take to turn things around."

Yet before we explore the steps Ted and Nancy can take to remedy their situation, it's important to understand what went wrong in their plan. At first glance, it might appear that their plan was basically good, and they merely were the victims of circumstances beyond their control. But upon closer examination, we can find important financial principles that were ignored or broken on their path to an economic tailspin.

Although it's common for people to blame their financial situation on external economic forces, this usually is a nearsighted view. In order to learn anything useful from Ted and Nancy's plight, we must look *deeper* than the external circumstances they faced due to the nation's economic downturn. The bursting of the "real estate bubble" may be a convenient excuse, but it's not the true *root* cause of their difficulties.

So what went wrong? What principles could Ted and Nancy have applied to avoid the destruction of their financial nest egg— everything they had worked so hard to accumulate?

Of course, Ted and Nancy's situation is not unique. Millions of households across our country are experiencing this same kind of personal economic quagmire. If we can understand the mess Ted and Nancy got into, we will have unraveled a mystery affecting countless other families.

Economic storms are bound to occur from time to time. However, they don't need to bring the kind of financial devastation experienced by Ted and Nancy. While there's no way to completely avoid the storms, we *can* sidestep most of the destruction if we apply the steps of the Economic Destiny Program.

For example, here are some basic principles you must understand:

1. Don't depend on the government or the stock market to determine your financial future.

2. Don't ever put all your financial eggs in one basket.

3. Don't ever delegate your financial decisions to someone else.

4. Do become knowledgeable of how money works.

5. Most importantly, count the total cost of your investment decisions before you make them. If you don't know what tax bracket you will be in by the time you need the money, then deferring taxes might not be your best choice.

Each of these five principles is based on a fundamental truth that is commonly ignored today. The fact is, you are *personally responsible* for the outcome of your financial decisions. You'll get nowhere by delegating responsibility—or blame—to the government, the stock market, or your financial advisor. It's *your* money, so you must learn how to handle it properly.

PROSPERING IN TOUGH FINANCIAL TIMES

There are practical steps you can take to experience financial success despite poor economic decisions you've made in the past. You can learn how to manage your existing resources and position yourself to be the lender instead of the borrower; this will put you in a unique position to take advantage of the financial opportunities you will encounter in any economy.

Before we move on to share the specifics of how you can become a wise investor, let's review the first six of the seven principles of the Economic Destiny Program:

- **PLAN AHEAD**
- **PAY YOURSELF FIRST (AFTER GIVING BACK TO GOD)**
- **SPEND WITHIN YOUR MEANS**
- **ELIMINATE DEBT**
- **TRANSFORM WASTE TO WEALTH**
- **BECOME A WISE INVESTOR**

With all the turmoil that occurred in the stock market during the 2008, 2009 and 2010 economic crisis, many people lost as much as 30% to 45% of the value of their retirement accounts. That's how much their mutual funds and other Wall Street investment products declined in a short period of time. The majority of those losses could have been avoided if the information contained in these pages was more widely known and practiced.

One of the main purposes for this book is to educate you on how to use stable, profitable and predictable Wall Street alternatives. The stock market is NOT the only, and clearly not the safest, place to invest your retirement savings. Fortunately, I'm able to recommend a number of stable alternatives for this purpose—and one of the key objectives must be to reduce your risks.

MINIMIZING YOUR RISKS

Ted and Nancy made several mistakes that cost them dearly. Too much of their nest egg was put into a basket which they had no control over: the two houses they built and their 401(k) accounts. They didn't realize it at the time, but these investments turned out to be risky and unstable.

Fortunately, there are time-tested, stable, reliable financial strategies that will allow you to fund a number of wealth-building accounts with minimal risks. These strategies will enable you to meet your short-term and long-term investment goals, without jeopardizing your principal.

It's likely that you've heard, and perhaps believed, the common myth that *less risk* means *less profitable*. This isn't necessarily true!

For example, you can structure a plan to implement the *IBC* plan described in chapter 14, which is completely in line with the principles taught in the Economic Destiny Program. These are the life-changing values I'm teaching in businesses, churches and communities all around the country.

My desire is to see your family, business, church and community...

- Break free from the bondage of debt

- Build a solid financial foundation

- Be positioned to be a blessing to others

- Leave a legacy to the next generation so they don't have to re-invent the wheel

Freedom is a key Biblical principle and a foundation stone to the birth of our nation. The Economic Destiny Program strives to keep freedom where it belongs—with *you*—so the next generation is born into a country that retains its foundation of faith, hope and charity. If these core values remain the focus of our lives, we'll inevitably experience a wellspring of blessings and prosperity from our Creator.

So no matter what the economic circumstances around you may be, I make you this pledge: *By applying the principles of the Economic Destiny Program, you can achieve economic success or an economic recovery in your household, church or business.*

CHANGING SURPLUS INTO WEALTH

KEY FINANCIAL PRINCIPLE: A SMALL SURPLUS OVER TIME BECOMES ABUNDANCE WHEN COUPLED WITH THE PROPER USE OF COMPOUND INTEREST.

Once you decide to establish your surplus savings account, you must organize your plans and make decisions that are consistent with your long-term financial goals. Your short-term goal is to make sure your basic living expenses are covered, but your ultimate long-term goal should be to make sure each dollar you earn is a permanent employee— working for you at all times, continually multiplying and increasing.

In order for this to happen, you will need to learn how to get the best possible return on your savings, with the minimum amount of risk. This requires an understanding of the basic principles of saving and investing, and how to use compound interest in your favor.

REMEMBER: God's economic system works on the principle of surplus. When we create a surplus, we must invest it wisely, guarding our resources from an undue risk of loss. Note that this principle runs contrary to the mainstream school of thought that taking greater risk with your investment dollars will ultimately bring you a greater return.

Solomon, who was the richest man who ever lived, warns in the Bible that we should avoid gambling and speculative investments. After his lifetime of amassing great wealth, he advises us that long-term prosperity comes through "steady plodding" rather than risk-taking:

Steady plodding brings prosperity, hasty speculation brings poverty (Proverbs 21:5 TLB).

There is another serious problem I have seen everywhere— savings are being put into risky investments that turn sour, and soon there is nothing left to pass on to one's son. The man who speculates is soon back to where he began—with nothing. This, as I said, is a very serious problem, for all his hard work has been for nothing; he has been working for the wind. It is all swept away (Ecclesiastes 5:13-16 TLB).

There is so much wisdom in these few verses! If we take this advice to heart, it will serve us well for a lifetime of God's favor on our work, earnings, savings and investments.

One of the main reasons many investments go bad is greed—the desire for a quick return or a much larger return than our efforts justify. For years we've been told that our retirement accounts invested in mutual funds, ETFs and other Wall Street products are certain to bring a great return over time—but is that really the truth?

The message of the financial firms is relentless, and often very appealing: *They promise that you'll come out better over the long haul if you simply put your money in their accounts and let them manage it for you.* However, a little research will show that *no one* can predict what an

151

investment will do with 100% accuracy. Despite the cockiness and bluster of many financial gurus, their actual performance seldom matches the hype.

So be a wise investor. Be careful when you hear wild promises of high rates of return. Consider your overall financial strategy instead of just focusing on the rate of return of a certain investment. In many cases, there are two sides of a coin when it comes to investments. By focusing only on the "speculative return" side of the investment, we can overlook negative factors on the other side, which are making our investment efforts futile in their final outcome.

This is depicted in the following illustration. By focusing only on increasing our wealth through making higher rates of returns,

we are just like the person who continues to poor more water into a bucket with holes hoping it will eventually somehow fill up.. Is this being a wise investor? Of course not. You must first plug the holes in your bucket! Then even if your contributions into the bucket slow down to a trickle, it will eventually fill up to over flowing.

ACTION STEPS:

1. COUNT THE COSTS ASSOCIATED WITH ALL YOUR INVESTMENTS: INTEREST PAID ON DEBT, FEES, PENALTIES, TAXES, AND OPPORTUNITY COSTS.

2. AVOID SPECULATIVE INVESTMENTS.

3. MANAGE YOUR OWN BUSINESS AFFAIRS.

4. LEARN SIMPLE, PREDICTABLE STRATEGIES TO ACCOMPLISH YOUR LONG-TERM FINANCIAL GOALS.

Developing a successful wealth-building plan involves two fundamental ingredients: *time* and *consistency*. So how can you make the best use of time and consistency in order to maximize your long-term investment strategy?

To receive the greatest long-term impact, here are some vital steps you must take:

- Educate yourself on how compound interest works.

- Develop strategies that are consistent with your long-term financial goals.

- Determine how much money you want to have available as supplemental income in the future (without market speculation).

- Set up your *IBC* plan (as described in chapter 14). Use this as your own credit facility to increase the compound interest you earn and decrease the compound interest you pay to financial institutions.

HOW FINANCIAL INSTITUTIONS MAKE MONEY

Financial planners, brokers, investment advisors and bankers make money in an assortment of ways, including commissions, fees, interest, or services sold. Whenever you buy or sell an investment, you pay the broker a transaction fee and/or commission. The broker makes money on each transaction, regardless of the financial results you receive.

Did you hear that? Whether the transactions they recommend result in a gain or loss for you, the brokers still make money.

That's why the cards are stacked against the average investor. In too many cases, the incentive is for the broker/planner/advisor to sell you whichever products pay them the most commission.

ACTION STEP: DON'T LEAVE YOUR FINANCIAL FUTURE IN THE HANDS OF SOMEONE ELSE, SUCH AS THE GOVERNMENT, YOUR FINANCIAL PLANNER, YOUR EMPLOYER, YOUR ADVISORS, YOUR COMPANY'S 401(K) ADMINISTRATOR, ETC.

A GOLDEN CALF CANNOT SAVE YOU

In my search for truth, I found a fallacy that began a short *37 years ago*. It involves a theme repeated throughout the land by radio and TV financial gurus spoken "with pride" under the guise of sound financial advice. Pride always makes me question things.

I desired to find out if this advice was time-tested, and here is what I discovered. This "new age" thinking runs contrary to the time-tested wisdom of the ages given to us over *2000 years ago* by Solomon (a man blessed with prosperity and abundance from the hand of his Creator). We've been trained to exchange for our *solid gold* for what amounts to *fool's gold,* and the deceptive mantra goes something like this:

"Max out your 401(k) contributions at work, and don't touch any of the money you accumulate. You shouldn't try to invest your retirement funds yourself, because you will surely blow it. You are stupid with money, so leave your financial decisions in the hands of an honest Wall Street investor to manage for you. They know what's best for you. Trust me in this, someday on the other side of the rainbow, your pot of gold will be there for you, overflowing with plenty!"

Is this really your only option? Do you really think this is sound advice?

The statements above should cause you to stop and think. Consider who you are and what kind of advice it is that would take you away from applying sound principles of finance. First and foremost, you are *not* stupid! You are a child of God, and if you apply His wisdom spoken from the lips of Solomon, you will be transformed into a wise investor.

Although a wise investor is not opposed to 401(k) plans, under the Economic Destiny Program you should focus more on low-risk or guaranteed options when contributing to these kinds of plans. For example, if you invest in a tax-deferred 401(k) at your work, it's usually best to invest up to the maximum percentage your employer matches. But if your employer does not contribute any matching funds, then a 401(k) is not the most efficient financial tool for a wise investor.

If your employer is matching your 401(k) contribution, here's what wise investors do in that scenario: They take the match and place their money in a guaranteed interest account or guaranteed bond. This way, they're getting a 100% return from the match, but never putting their original principal at risk in a Wall Street mutual fund. Their 401(k) management fees will most likely be much less, and they will only pay on the backside of their investment in the form of the taxes they deferred.

Although a wise investor ordinarily does NOT attempt to multiply wealth by deferring taxes into an unpredictable future, there's an exception when the employer matches your contribution. Rather than following the path of risky speculation, this approach employs the Biblical principle of "steady plodding." It almost always creates a better result than risking your own principal in hopes of a greater return in the future.

Most people place their 401(k) investments primarily in products called no-load mutual funds. These funds are usually a mix of growth stocks, and since little or no commission is required up front, your entire investment goes to work for you immediately. This is generally a better scenario than paying commissions up-front to an advisor and then only receiving returns on the money left over after the commissions are paid. But although this sounds good in theory, there's another half of the story you need to understand...

THE TRUE COST OF A 401(K)

Let's take a look at the big picture, so we can count the entire cost of a tax-deferred 401(k) mutual fund strategy. The profits gained in a 401(k) are tax-deferred, meaning you don't pay taxes now but sometime out in the future. What does that really mean? Let me share a hypothetical story to show you how this works.

If you went to the bank to get a $100,000 loan, one of the first questions you would ask is, "What's the interest rate?" This is a logical question to ask, because you would want to know how much the loan is going to cost you.

The second question you would ask is, "What's the term of the loan?" Again, this is a crucial question, because you'll want to know when you have to pay the loan back.

But what if the banker said in response to your two questions, "We don't know the interest rate we're going to charge you, and we don't know when we will need the money back. Just go ahead and take the loan, and we'll let you know how much you owe us sometime in the future."

Would you take out a loan like that—with several of the key terms unknown? No way!

Although this example may seem absurd, this is exactly what you're doing with the government when investing your money into a 401(k) or some other kind of tax-deferred investment plan. The profits gained are taxed in the *future*. So if taxes go *up* in the future, you lose.

"But Jeff," you may argue, "if taxes go *down* or stay the *same*, I will win rather than lose."

Yes, that's half true. However, be honest with yourself: Do you think taxes will go up in the future or down? If you invest in a tax-deferred investment, you're setting yourself up to pay taxes on the harvest (a larger amount) at an unknown tax rate in the future instead of on the seed (the smaller amount) at a rate you now know. **Figure 9.0** illustrates this point.

FIGURE **9.0**

Harvest

Seeds

Figure 9.0 poses a question every wise investor needs to ask. If you were an apple farmer, would you rather pay taxes on the four seeds you once planted, or would you rather defer the taxes and pay them on **all** the apples your four seeds eventually produced year after year? Of course, you wouldn't want to pay taxes on the entire harvest—a much larger amount. It would be far better to only pay taxes on the seeds.

REMEMBER: You will pay future taxes on any gains you have in your tax-deferred plans. But it's impossible to know for sure how high those taxes will be or what tax bracket you will be in. Wise investors avoid gambling their money away on future uncertainties. Your goal in the Economic Destiny Program is to move your money from accounts that are "forever taxed" to accounts that are "never taxed."

 **ACTION STEP:** BECOME FAMILIAR WITH HOW MONEY WORKS. EDUCATE YOURSELF ON THE DIFFERENT TYPES OF INVESTMENT VEHICLES THAT ARE SUITABLE TO YOUR CIRCUMSTANCES AND INCOME GOALS.

THE POWER OF COMPOUND INTEREST

Albert Einstein once observed: "Compound interest is one of the most powerful forces in the universe. Those who understand it will earn it, and those that don't will pay it."

Perhaps you've heard the question asked, "Which would you rather have—$50,000 immediately or the compound interest on $.01 that would double in value each day for a month?" The average person would take the $50,000, but I would like you to do this exercise for yourself. Which is greater, and which one would you take? If you said the penny, you're becoming a wise investor. If you took the $50,000, you just gave up $1,292,177.28 and need to understand how compound interest works!

It's vital that you learn how to put the power of compound interest to work in your favor instead of having it always work against you. Wise Investors call this "living on the right side of interest."

The Rule of 72 is a helpful tool that demonstrates how the power of compound interest can work for you or against you. The Rule of 72 allows you to calculate the amount of time it will take for your money to double using compound interest. This works by dividing 72 by the interest rate you are able to get. For example, if you are receiving 4% interest on your investment your money will double every 18 years (72 divided by 4 = 18). Notice the chart below.

Interest Rate	Number of Years to Double
4%	18
8%	9
12%	6
18%	4
24%	3

Based on the Rule of 72, if you invested $1,000 at 9% interest when you were age 25, compound interest would cause your money to double every eight years. By age 65 you would have $32,000. In other words, if you only invested $1,000 (with no additional investment), you would end up with $32,000—which is *32 times* your original investment!

By using the Rule of 72, you can easily calculate how many years it will take for your money to double. The higher the interest rate, the faster your money grows.

Wise investors understand the power of compound interest and will stop and think to themselves, "If the power of compound interest can make me wealthy, then what is happening to me if I continue paying interest? What if I stopped paying interest to others and began paying interest to myself for the next 30 years?"

When wise investors boldly face this crossroads, a powerful lesson is learned, and a whole new world of opportunities begins to open up.

ACTION STEP: USE AUTOMATIC PAYROLL DEDUCTIONS TO START FUNDING YOUR OWN BANKING/SAVINGS SYSTEM. BY INVESTING A SMALL AMOUNT OF MONEY OVER A PERIOD OF TIME AND LEARNING HOW TO PAY YOURSELF INTEREST, EVEN A MODEST CONTRIBUTION CAN GROW INTO A SUBSTANTIAL AMOUNT OF WEALTH. THE KEY IS STARTING NOW AND BEING CONSISTENT.

SAVING VS. INVESTING

Saving and investing are not the same thing! Investing is risking your original principal for a possible greater return in the future. Saving, on the other hand, means earning interest and sometimes dividends (returns) without putting your original principal contributions at risk. Put another way: Saving is the accumulation of money you do not want to lose.

Matthew 25:27 makes a direct reference to the fact that we should save money and expect to make interest on it: "You should have put my money on deposit with the bankers, so that when I returned I would have received it back with interest." A good steward understands the power of interest and applies it in his favor. It's a mismanagement of God's resources to waste your time and money paying interest instead of earning interest.

KEY FINANCIAL PRINCIPLE: IT'S WISE TO SAVE A PORTION OF YOUR INCOME FOR THE FUTURE DURING YOUR PRODUCTIVE YEARS, SO THAT YOU HAVE ADEQUATE PROVISIONS DURING TIMES WHEN YOU MIGHT NOT BE ABLE TO WORK.

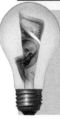

ACTION STEP: USE THE POWER OF COMPOUND INTEREST TO WORK FOR YOU INSTEAD OF AGAINST YOU AS YOU IMPLEMENT YOUR LONG-TERM INVESTMENT STRATEGY.

BUILDING A MILLION-DOLLAR RETIREMENT ACCOUNT

As you discipline yourself to set aside a little from each paycheck and then allow compound interest to work on your behalf, you can easily accumulate a retirement account in excess of a million dollars over your lifetime. However, you have to get started *now*, for it takes both time, consistency, and the proper strategy to achieve this kind of result.

The key is not a large income. Even a modest income will work. All it takes to create a big retirement account is consistently saving a small amount from each paycheck.

But you have to avoid procrastination. Many people figure they don't need to do financial planning until they have a large estate. This is completely backwards! You are highly unlikely to *ever* become wealthy if you take that approach. You are responsible to be a good steward of the money God blesses you with, and that requires planning and saving *now*, not later.

KEY FINANCIAL PRINCIPLE: NEVER PUT OFF UNTIL TOMORROW WHAT YOU CAN DO TODAY.

Have you ever heard of the "Tomorrow Diet"? Many of us have pledged to start a diet "tomorrow" (or at some later date), but that rarely ever happens. In the same way, you must avoid the common trap of thinking you'll get around to saving and investing *later* to build your retirement accounts. Compound interest can provide you with powerful benefits, so the sooner you start using it the better.

KEY FINANCIAL PRINCIPLE: SAVE AND INVEST IN PLANS THAT PRODUCE GUARANTEED AND PREDICTABLE OUTCOMES.

Ask anyone who had their entire retirement account invested in the stock market during the 2008/2009 market correction, and they will tell you stories of big losses. For those close to retirement, these were *life-altering* losses. Some people have had to postpone their retirement for 5, 10, or even 15 years. It would be one thing if this was just a temporary and short-term dip in people's 401(k) s, IRAs, SEPs, or Mutual Fund accounts. But for many, it's possible their retirement accounts will *never* return to where they were in 2008 prior to the correction.

While some would argue that the very nature of investing is taking *some* risk for a higher return in the future, it doesn't have to be this way! If those who lost substantial sums in the 2008 Wall Street meltdown could go back and do it over again, what do you think they would rather have had—a return "on" their investments or a return "of" their investments?

PREDICTABLE INVESTMENTS?

When you hear the words "predictable" and "investment" in the same sentence, it sounds like an oxymoron—a complete contradiction in terms. But by using the time-tested principles of the Economic Destiny Program along with the *IBC* plan I will be describing in chapter 14, this is entirely possible.

The *real* contradiction is allowing someone else to gamble with your money, hoping they will look out for your best interests. Yet this is exactly what so many choose to do.

Risk is not all bad, but it's far better to calculate the risk/reward/ loss *before* putting yourself and your finances at any level of risk. It's important that you determine your risk up front and make your investments in line with God's plan for your life.

Diversification of your investments is generally a good thing, and some IRA / 401(k) accounts and investment portfolios are somewhat designed that way. However, as you may have already experienced, even diversified investments carry no guarantees against loss or a greater return in the future.

Another question to ask yourself is this: Do you really know who is managing your investments or how diversified your funds really are? Is your financial advisor truly interested in your family's goals and dreams? Do you have a contract with them that protects you from the loss of your original principal balance—or is your entire financial destiny in someone else's hands, with no guarantee to hedge against total loss? Although you might think a guarantee like this is impossible, in the next chapter I'll explain in more detail how this can be done using the *IBC* plan.

The *IBC* plan is based on time-tested fundamental banking rules. Why is understanding the fundamentals of banking an important part of your economic destiny? For many reasons, but let me briefly expose you to 2 fundamental banking rules all Wise Investors follow:

RULE NUMBER 1. NEVER LOSE YOUR PRINCIPAL.

RULE NUMBER 2. NEVER DISOBEY RULE NUMBER 1.

Applying core banking principles have brought prosperity to only a privileged few for thousands of years. But as **Figure 10.0** shows, there's an enormous gap between those who understand the principles and those who don't.

If we are going to be good economists in our own homes and businesses, we must understand how to implement basic banking principles. Sadly, these principles are no longer taught in schools, so we must find other ways to learn them.

Looking at the average financial condition of Americans after the age of 65 tells us that it's not what we know that hurts us, it's what we think we know that just ain't so.

Figure 10.0 on the next page shows the huge contrast between those who have learned the principles of a wise investor and those who have not. At age 65, 36% of us are still working, and 54% of us are broke. Only 4% are financially secure by age 65 (not needing the government to provide for their basic needs).

These are facts we cannot just ignore. The bottom line is this: Millions of Americans unnecessarily fall short of their full economic potential. While the question used to be "When will you retire?" the new question is "Will you *ever* be able to retire?"

FIGURE 10.0 – FINANCIAL STATISTICS OF AMERICANS AT AGE 65

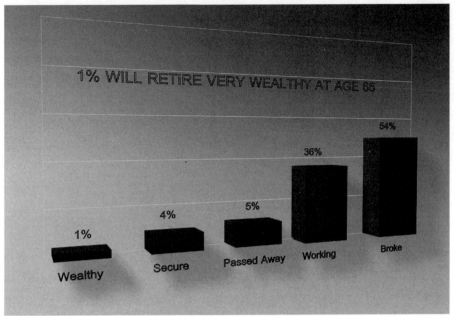

Maybe **Figure 10.0** can be better explained by an analogy. Picture 20,000 teens in a football stadium, half on each side. If you asked them, "By a show of hands, how many of you are going to be financially secure by the time you're 65?" it's likely that nearly all the hands would go up.

Now what if you broke the news that statistically 54% of them would be broke at age 65. Then you asked: "I want each of you to point to the side of the stadium that's going to be broke at age 65. It's going to be one side or the other, but not both." Guess what would happen. Almost everyone would point to the *other* side!

You see, we all tend to rationalize, "NOT ME!" But it's a fact that only 4% will take proper action and learn how to become wise investors and "good and faithful stewards" of their resources.

An extensive report by KRON4 TV's "Rob Black & Your Money" (4/5/06) made the startling observation:

Most Americans think they'll be able to retire comfortably, but most aren't saving nearly enough to meet that goal. Sixty-eight percent of workers are confident they will have adequate funds for a comfortable retirement. And yet, more than half of those workers have saved less than $25,000 for retirement. Only 20% of Americans have saved $100,000 or more. And only 10% of Americans have amassed retirement savings of $200,000.

In order to achieve your financial goals, it's crucial that you increase your economic literacy, become familiar with the available financial tools, and work with trusted advisors who can help you navigate through unfamiliar territory. The goal is to grow your surplus without putting your investment at risk.

Remember the story of Ted and Nancy at the beginning of the chapter? They invested in real estate and the stock market, and both of those choices put their original principal at risk. They lost control over their investments and couldn't access their own funds without encountering one or more adverse consequences:

- THE NEED TO GET SOMEONE ELSE'S PERMISSION

- PAYING THE COSTS OF REFINANCING

- LIQUIDATING AT A LOSS

- PAYING HIGH PENALTIES FOR ACCESSING THEIR OWN MONEY WHEN THEY REALLY NEEDED IT

- PAYING "OPPORTUNITY COSTS" EVERY DAY THEIR MONEY WAS IN SOMEONE ELSE'S HANDS

If Ted and Nancy would have redirected those dollars into an *IBC* plan and "paid themselves first" for just 20 years, they would have amassed a tax-free supplemental retirement income of over $95,000 per year, payable every year from age 61 to 95. How different their lives would be today if they had reevaluated their goals and made use of a powerful *IBC* plan. Instead of leaving a paid-off home valued at $345,000 to their children, they could have left a total legacy somewhere in the $1.7 million range.

ON WALL STREET, BANKING PRINCIPLES DON'T APPLY

Wise investors know that banking is a process, not a product. Bankers follow known rules that are based on contractual certainties, not future speculations or charts based on past performance. To engage in speculative investments would be breaking their own principles.

Even in light of the great Wall Street meltdown, investment bankers, financial planners, IRA and 401(k) administrators continue to operate in a world of speculative uncertainties. Why? For many reasons. But for starters, consider this: They're not playing with their own money, they're playing with *yours*!

A wise investor takes several important pieces of knowledge into account:

1. What the fund's prospectus says

2. How much money they'll be allowing someone else to invest for them

3. The fact that projected returns on their investments are based on "past performance" only

4. How the Average Annual Rate of Return on a fund's prospectus is calculated

Figure 11.0 Shows how a basic Average Annual Rate of Return over 4 years is calculated

FIGURE **11.0**

$200,000 Year One	$200,000 Year Three	**$100,000**
+100% -50%	+100% -50% =	25% Average Annual Return
Day One $100,000	Year Two $100,000	Year Four $100,000

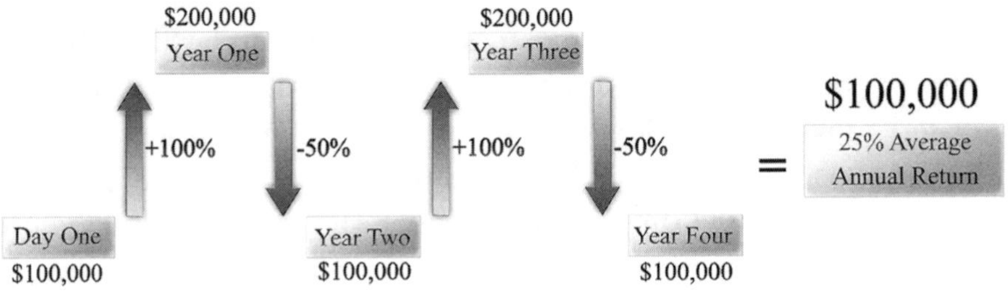

This illustration shows that you started with $100,000 to invest, and you had a 100% gain in year one. This grew your original investment to $200,000. But then the following year your investment had a 50% loss, bringing you back to where you originally started. This same pattern continued for the next three years.

The financial experts would proudly tell you they were able to get you an average return of 25% over a four-year period. But don't be fooled by what an "average return on investment" really means. As you can see, four years went by and you have the *exact same amount of money* you originally started with! If that's not scary enough, just think what kind of percentage gain you would have to achieve to get back to even if you lost *more* than 50% in any of those years. To sum it up, the only person who made any money during those 4 years was the person in charge of managing your money, yet you were the one who took all the risk!

ACTION STEP: LEARN HOW TO PROPERLY CALCULATE A RATE OF RETURN ON YOUR INVESTMENT.

It's time to expose the misleading financial messages concerning rates of return and diversified investment portfolios:

- "If you invest over the long haul, the stock market will inevitably bring you a greater return on your investment."

- "If you time the market correctly and invest in the right type of fund or product, then you can rest well, knowing that your assets are growing and will be there when it's time for you to retire."

Hold on a second! Do these commonly stated financial precepts really make any sense? They're just about as logical as saying, "If you invest in the same set of golf clubs as Phil Mickelson used to win the 2010 Masters Golf Tournament, your odds are better that you can win the Masters too."

The problem is that we tend to focus too much on the *tools* or *products* we use rather than the soundness of our *strategy*. If your stream of retirement income depended on choosing between Phil Mickelson's *clubs* or his *ability*, which would you choose? The answer is obvious.

Dalbar Associates, a trusted market research firm, conducted a study analyzing investor behavior. The study reported that during the years 1983 to 2002, the average investor received a return of only 2.57%—a return that was even lower than the 3.14% average inflation rate for the same 20-year period. The average investor actually *lost ground* during this 20-year span!

Perhaps you think this study just picked a random period when the stock market wasn't doing well. Quite the contrary! During this 20-year period, the U.S. had the greatest Bull Market in stocks ever. The S&P 500 Index had an average annual return of over 12% for the period. So even though the overall market did well, the net return for most investors was horrible.

ROLLERCOASTERS ARE FOR AMUSEMENT PARKS, NOT INVESTMENTS!

People invest in Wall Street hoping they'll have a generous return over time, and they're cheered on by radio and TV financial gurus who say: *"The smartest thing you can do right now is hold on to your investments. Instead of cashing out your stocks now, ride this market rollercoaster to the very end. After all, the only way to get hurt on a roller coaster is to jump off!"*

Statements like this run contrary to the truth of Scripture and contrary to sound advice. The Bible cites "steady plodding" and having control over your investments as the best path to lasting abundance. **Have you really taken a close look at the performance of the Dow Jones Industrial Average during the past 10 years?**

Figure 12.0 shows the difference between "steady plodding" and chasing high rates of return in the stock market (which the Bible describes as "hasty speculation").

Figure 12.0 shows you what the stock market rollercoaster is really like. If you were diversified in the market and reviewed your rates of returns over a 10-year span of time, what would that look like from a profit perspective? The bottom line (DJIA) is what would happen to your money if invested in the market under someone else's control.

According to the data, if you were diversified in the market from October 1, 1999 to October 1, 2009 via a 401(k), IRA, or mutual fund, your investment would encounter many ups and downs during that period. A full 10 years after your original investment, your $11,497 would actually have fallen to $10,471! You not only would have lost money, but you also would have lost 10 years of your investing lifetime. That's one step forward and two steps back—something Wise Investors call the Wall Street waltz.

Figure 12.0 also shows you what happens if the same amount of money is invested in a Certificate of Deposit. As surprising as it may seem, during that same period of time, the corner bank could have done better than Wall Street.

FIGURE **12.0**

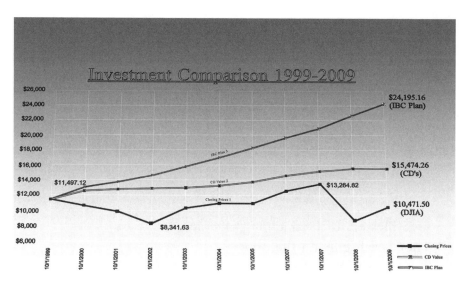

But look what happens under the *IBC* plan. The results speak for themselves. As the Bible predicts, steady plodding will bring prosperity, while hasty market speculation will bring poverty and a loss on your investment (Proverbs 21:5 TLB).

A LEGACY FOR YOUR FAMILY

As I've repeatedly mentioned, planning is a vital key to long-term financial success. But this planning shouldn't be limited to your retirement income—it must include your estate plan too.

Inheritance for your children: Your family is your responsibility, and leaving them a financial legacy requires creating a sound, guaranteed economic plan and sticking to it. One of your primary purposes for building wealth should be to leave a financial legacy for your family—instead of leaving them with the hardships created by debts and estate tax repercussions. **AND REMEMBER:** The best legacy you can leave is to teach your family how to build wealth by using the principles outlined in the Economic Destiny Program.

ACTION STEP: MAKE INVESTMENTS THAT WILL PAY CONTINUAL RETURNS.

Charitable giving: As you execute your plan for saving and investing, you will reap an ever-larger surplus. Part of becoming a wise investor is to invest your time and efforts into the lives of others and into humanitarian projects that need your support.

The Message paraphrase of Psalm 112:8-9 describes the blessed life of a person who is generous with the poor:

Ever blessed, relaxed among enemies,
They lavish gifts on the poor—
A generosity that goes on, and on, and on.
An honored life! A beautiful life!

This is the kind of "beautiful life" God wants *you* to have!

ACTION STEP: ESTABLISH AN ACTION PLAN THAT INCLUDES PLANS FOR YOUR FAMILY TO RECEIVE A FINANCIAL LEGACY AND FOR NUMEROUS PEOPLE TO BE IMPACTED BY YOUR CHARITABLE GIFTS.

DEVELOPING ACCOUNTABILITY

Accountability and consistency are vital keys to success in any area of our lives. If we are going to attain our financial goals, we must keep them in sight at all times. You need someone to assist you in keeping your financial goals on track.

ACTION STEP: NEVER GET JUST ONE OPINION IN FINANCIAL MATTERS. THE SCRIPTURES SAY, "WHERE THERE IS NO COUNSEL, THE PEOPLE FALL; BUT IN THE MULTITUDE OF COUNSELORS THERE IS SAFETY" (PROVERBS 11:14).

I recommend that you employ a financial coach who is familiar with the principles and practical applications outlined in the Economic Destiny Program. The Economic Destiny Mentoring Program was created so you can hit your goals with precision, so your daily decisions will be consistent with your long-term wealth-building strategy and your written financial goals.

ACTION STEP: ESTABLISH AN ACCOUNTABILITY GROUP AND A FINANCIAL MENTORING TEAM YOU CAN TRUST.

The Economic Destiny Mentorship Program is committed to assisting you in achieving your personal financial victories in line with God's purpose for your life. It's my hope that your transformed economic destiny will in turn motivate you to be a blessing in the lives of others (Genesis 12:2). When you do so, the Bible makes an astounding promise:

> **God is able to make all grace abound toward you, that you, always having all sufficiency in all things, may have abundance for every good work (2 Corinthians 9:8).**

It's important that your financial mentor understands your desire to make a difference in the lives of others. He or she should stand on a firm foundation of Biblical wisdom and be able to sharpen your financial focus "as iron sharpens iron" (Proverbs 27:17).

It is critical that you surround yourself with people who demonstrate commitment, strength, honesty and integrity. The Bible warns that "evil company corrupts good habits" (1 Corinthians 15:33), it promises that "he who walks with wise men will be wise" (Proverbs 13:20).

CONCLUSIONS

To be a wise investor following the Economic Destiny Program, you must:

1. Maintain as much control as possible over your investments.

2. Make it your primary objective to maintain your principal and receive a substantial return.

3. Avoid transferring more of your wealth to the government and banks than you need to.

4. Make sure your money is continually working for you and compounding.

5. Understand and implement strategies that will help you grow your wealth and protect your family's wealth for generations to come.

So how does one begin to build wealth without taking on risk and without losing it to taxes, interest, fees, and market cycles? In the next chapter we are going to learn about the most important business in the world, banking! If that word doesn't excite you, here's my guarantee: by the time you're done with the next chapter it will. Banking is not a product but a process—combine that process with a good product and a proven financial strategy and you will be well on your way to understanding the secrets of Wise Investors who have discovered the power of accomplishing their financial goals by becoming their own bankers!

Chapter 14

BECOMING A WISE BANKER
DISCOVERING A WALL STREET ALTERNATIVE

"You finance everything you buy—you either pay interest
to someone else, or you give up interest you could have
earned otherwise." —R. Nelson Nash

"Truth will always be truth, regardless of lack of understanding,
disbelief or ignorance." —W. Clement Stone

A S A SOCIETY, WE'VE INCREASINGLY fused the concepts of "saving" and "investing." However, as I mentioned in the last chapter, these are two very distinct terms.

By failing to understand the difference between saving and investing, we've reaped a number of negative consequences. Many people have been hooked on the pursuit of quick returns, especially if many of their saving years have already passed them by. But instead of producing quick wealth, this impatient quest usually results in people's wealth being swept away by unnecessary fees, commissions, and Wall Street losses. And in many cases these losses are never recovered.

Compound interest on savings takes time. It's the exact *opposite* of "get rich quick." No matter how hard you try to reword it, fuse it, or redefine it, the truth of Scripture remains: "Steady plodding brings prosperity, and hasty speculation brings poverty" (Proverbs 21:5 TLB).

As I shared in the last chapter, the best time to start building wealth through the miracle of compound interest is *as soon as possible*! But if you're starting late in the game, don't despair. In all likelihood, you *still* have an ample opportunity to grow and preserve a substantial nest egg. If you are willing to commit yourself to systematic saving and investing for the future, there are reliable financial tools and time-tested financial strategies that can enable compound interest to build quickly, earn significant returns, and avoid putting any of your principal at risk in the process.

But in order to do this, you will need to focus more on your long-term financial strategy than on the latest and greatest financial product. Instead of chasing unrealistic returns, which are unsustainable over the long haul, there's a better approach for building wealth. In this chapter I'll reveal how combining the right products and right strategies will yield amazing benefits and preserve your family's wealth though multiple generations.

REGAINING LOST GROUND

After reading the last chapter, you may be thinking, "That's great, Jeff. I wish I would have known about the power of compound interest a lot sooner. I'm now far past the age of a young adult and need to make up for lost time. Is there anything I still can do?"

If you're already in your 50s, 60s or even 70s, you may conclude that time is not on your side. However, there *are* ways you can protect, accelerate and compound your growth while protecting your principal from Wall Street fluctuations and government taxes. You also can begin to exponentially multiply your gains by avoiding ongoing unnecessary negative wealth transfers due to interest, capital gains taxes, income taxes, estate taxes, fees and penalties.

If this sounds too good to be true, it's not. You really *can* have total control of your financial outcomes, without taking market risks. It's not only *possible* to come out way ahead of the masses; you're *guaranteed* to have this kind of result if you follow the right financial strategies. Yes, there are time-tested strategies that can help you regain lost ground on your surplus. In fact, you may still be able to grow such a large surplus that future generations will be impacted by your faithfulness and generosity.

ONE OF THE TOOLS USED BY WISE INVESTORS OF ALL AGES AND ECONOMIC LEVELS IS A TIME-TESTED MULTIGENERATIONAL FINANCIAL STRATEGY CALLED THE *"INFINITE BANKING CONCEPT."*

This incredible concept was discovered by a forestry engineer named R. Nelson Nash. By the nature of his education and acquired skills, Nelson was trained to think long-term—past the "right now" and far into future generations. Forestry engineers study the preservation of natural resources, and they find ways to recycle nature's gifts so that generations not yet born will continue to be blessed—thanks, in part, to careful planning by the engineers.

Multigenerational forestry planning requires diligent actions and precise calculations as to the past, present and future consumption of natural resources. A spoonful of patience and an unselfish heart is the minimum required for excelling at this kind of work.

In the early 1980s, Nelson told his story in what became an underground book classic, selling more than 200,000 copies: *Becoming Your Own Banker®*. He described how he discovered the INFINITE BANKING CONCEPT® (*IBC*) over a period of many, many months. Many of his insights came at 3:00 to 4:00 a.m. while kneeling in desperate prayer: "Lord, please show me a way out of this financial nightmare I've created for myself."

To his surprise, Nelson sensed God telling him, "You're standing in the midst of everything it takes to get out—but you don't see it because you look at things like everyone else."

Nelson's moment of revelation, and his faithfulness to respond to God's calling, has resulted in countless lives being set free by discovering a way out of bondage and back into a position of control over their financial resources. Nelson says, "The INFINITE BANKING CONCEPT is an exercise in imagination, reason, logic and prophecy!"[1]

The basis of the *IBC* concept is a financial product originally designed by two Scottish clergymen who were concerned for the well-being of widows and orphans. They developed a financial tool that most people think they understand—but it's the most misunderstood and poorly explained financial product in the world.

This product is not new. It's been around for over 200 years. But unfortunately, the so-called "experts" in the financial industry have refused to see or acknowledge the infinite possibilities it holds. What I have personally discovered through my exhaustive course of due-diligence is that it not only is one of the safest places to put your savings, but it also enables you to create your own privatized credit facility and build long-term wealth that can last for multiple generations. How could one product do all this? There are many reasons, but here are just a few:

- The interest you earn is contractually guaranteed.

- The interest you earn is much higher than most banks pay.

- The interest and dividends earned are not subject to capital gains taxes.[2]

- When you take money out, it can come out tax-free.

- Your principal is protected from equity loss.

- The money is safe from bankruptcy and creditors.[3]

- There are no restrictions on how you can use the money.

- There are no restrictions on the amount of contributions.

- You have liquidity, use, and total control of your money at all times.

---

1   Used with permission granted from R. Nelson Nash
2   Under IRS Tax Code Dividends are considered a return of preminum
3   Each state has different laws so check with your tax agency for details on laws in your state.

- You're enabled to build a multigenerational financial strategy, and the value of your estate passes to your heirs tax-free.

- The money can be drawn at any age, penalty-free, when properly drawn, is *never* taxed.

- You can create your own credit facility enabling you to Become Your Own Banker.

- Most important, you're enabled to tap into the power of the INFINITE BANKING CONCEPT!

How do these features compare with the type of account where you've put *your* savings and retirement funds into? I think you'll see, the INFINITE BANKING CONCEPT® surpasses the benefits of any other kind of wealth-building and wealth-preservation strategy you have been exposed to.

LEARNING POINT: MOST OF US SPEND OUR LIVES PAYING INTEREST TO OTHERS BUT SPEND VERY LITTLE TIME LEARNING HOW TO GET OTHERS TO PAY INTEREST TO US.

WHAT IS THIS AMAZING TOOL?

What kind of product can provide all of these benefits? Before you guess, you need to ask yourself this question: If what you thought was true turned out to be false, then when would you want to know about it?

You might be surprised to find out that you will only find these benefits in a specially structured, dividend-paying, cash-value, whole life insurance policy.

"Hmmm…" you might be thinking, "I've been told that whole life insurance is the kind of insurance only purchased by the wealthy. And I've also been told that whole life insurance is a terrible investment and a bad place to put your money." Well, you might be pleased to find out that what you have been told is absolutely 100% correct!

But in order to understand why I laid out all those benefits, you must look more at what you have *not* been told. Because it's what you *haven't* been told by the financial industry that could hurt you even more!

First of all, this type of life insurance is not just used by the wealthy, but it's used by those who want to *become* wealthy. The wealthy understand how money works, and they understand how powerful and efficient this financial tool is for growing and preserving their wealth.

The average person is never taught the financial secrets learned by the wealthiest 3% of the population. That's why it's often been said that if all the wealth of the wealthy was redistributed to the poor and the middle class, it would only take 10 years or less for all of the wealth to end up back in the hands of the wealthy! Why?

There are many reasons for this, but one of the most obvious is that the wealthy understand how to multiply their resources through banking, and they apply those principles to every financial decision they make. They understand that money is a resource just like water, and just like water, all money comes from one place and it always returns to that same place.

With the proper understanding of this knowledge—that all the money in the world comes from the same pool, and that you put your money into that pool when you deposit your income into your bank account—you will begin to see a missing link in your financial literacy. Then you'll be astonished what that missing link can do for you.

UNDERSTANDING THE MONEY POOL

When you put your money in the pool, your bank sells your money to another financial institution, and that other financial institution turns around and sells it back to you at a premium. How? They send you a credit card offer at a 14% interest rate to loan you money, and where did they *get* the money? From the same pool of money where you deposited your paycheck! *Ouch!*

So in reality the credit card company took your money from the pool, marked it up, and sold it back to you! *Every dollar* you give your bank or financial institution is lent back to you on your mortgage, your cars, your education loans, or your business lines of credit, and they expect you to give them *3 dollars* back!

Unless reversed, this cycle of "not drinking from your own pool" will keep you from building any significant long-term wealth. If you understand and see that this cycle is simply madness, you should be thinking, "How can I put an end to this?"

I'll reveal just how that's possible using a proven Wall Street Alternative banking strategy. Instead of continually losing your wealth by drinking from someone else's pool, you'll discover how to build your own pool and learn a revolutionary strategy to recycle your own water (wealth) and build lasting reserves. But you must first be willing to transform your thinking into that of a steward, a cultivator, and a preservationist who truly wants to maximize his or her resources.

Let's begin with this example: A farmer's water rights are critical to his ability to grow crops and gain an abundant harvest year after year. Wise farmers have learned how to capture the water that flows though their fields and recycle it back into their cropland. If they depended only on new water to fall on their land to grow their crops they would eventually starve.

Electrical engineers apply the same principles in developing hydroelectric dams. They don't just rely on new water to flow over the dam to create energy. They use the energy created to pump some of the water back up into the reservoir and let that water recycle back over the dam to create even more energy. Apply this same principle to your own personal economy, and you can't help but continue to compound and multiply your resources.

LENDER OR SLAVE—WHICH ARE YOU?

Contrary to what you might have been told, you cannot be both the slave *and* the master—you will be one or the other, but not both.

One might say, "I don't borrow anymore. I finally have financial peace, because I'm debt free!!" Let me be the first to congratulate

179

you on that accomplishment, but before you rest too long in that spot, it's critical to understand that being debt-free is not a destination, it's only the half-way point.

Your journey to your divine economic destiny requires you to complete the entire course, and that means thinking beyond yourself and even beyond this present generation. Your economic destiny is eternal, and your legacy is to impact nations and the generations that follow you. Your destiny is freedom and abundance, and this is not just for yourself.

You've probably heard the misleading old slogan, "Cash is king." However, the U.S. dollar has depreciated in value by 90 to 95% since 1913. This means your cash asset is actually a *depreciating* asset, so it takes more and more cash to provide for your family and support the causes that are really making a difference in this world.

If you're not in debt, that's a good thing, for Deuteronomy 28 says a borrower becomes a slave to the lender. But that's not *all* it says. In order for the truth to set you free, your mind must be renewed by it, and your mind cannot be fully renewed unless you are taught the *whole* truth in its proper context. If you read the entire passage, you will see that it says you not only are to be a lender, but you are to lend to *many nations*! Deuteronomy 28 is not just saying you can avoid being the *tail*, but it's also telling you to be the *head*.

So how does one become the head, and how does one become the lender? Banking. As R. Nelson Nash points out:

"CAREERS AND BUSINESSES COME AND GO, BUT BANKING IS ETERNAL."

Avoiding the cash-is-king "arrival syndrome" takes a broader understanding of your divine economic destiny. Your economic destiny is not just in overcoming bondage to debt, it's about becoming a *conqueror* in all things eternal. Nelson received the surprising revelation that there's something "eternal" about banking.

Remember that the root meaning of the word *interest* is "to give birth." The main component of lending is to create interest, "giving birth" to growth and multiplication, seedtime and harvest.

Remember this: Banks lend! They do not invest. Lending creates interest, and interest multiplies. Interest continues giving birth to more, and it never stops. Lending puts a natural law in motion, and the multiplier effect starts the moment the lending begins. But how can you lend if you don't own a bank? Now that is a great question.

As you might imagine, it's not an easy task to open up a bank. Few people have the necessary time, money and guaranteed resources they need in order to get started. Before the government regulators grant a charter for a new bank, the bank owners must meet difficult requirements, showing guaranteed assets of a specified value.

The new bank seeking a charter needs to show the banking authorities a certain amount of "tier one" assets such as these:

1. PRECIOUS METALS, SUCH AS GOLD, SILVER AND PLATINUM

2. CASH, USUALLY IN THE FORM OF DIFFERENT TYPES OF CURRENCY, AND LOTS OF IT

3. GUARANTEED BONDS, SUCH AS U.S. TREASURY BONDS

4. (BOLI)

You might have some of these "tier one" assets in your portfolio, and that's a good thing. But do you have BOLI in your portfolio? My guess is, if you've been listening to the "financial experts," you don't have this.

BOLI is the acronym for Bank Owned Life Insurance. BOLI is not just *any* kind of life insurance. Just like any other Tier 1 assets a bank holds, it must be a guaranteed asset. The banks don't buy term insurance and invest the difference; they buy dividend-paying whole life insurance from a mutual company and invest the whole thing. Understand this and you are on your way to *real* financial literacy.

Wise investors do not do what the banks *tell* them to do, but they mimic exactly what the banks actually *do*. By doing what banks have done for years, you are taking wealth mastery tips from the wealthiest institutions in the world. Who better to mimic? The guy who made it big gambling in the stock or real estate markets once or twice, or a 5,000-year-old institution that still holds most of the world's wealth in its own reservoir?

Doing what banks do will set you on the path to achieving your economic destiny. This is why it's critical to understand this vital principle shared by R. Nelson Nash:

YOU FINANCE **EVERYTHING** YOU BUY.
YOU EITHER PAY INTEREST TO SOMEONE ELSE,
OR YOU PAY CASH AND GIVE UP THE INTEREST
YOU OTHERWISE COULD HAVE EARNED.

Because interest works 24 hours a day, 7 days a week, 365 days a year until the world stops turning, every dollar you pay to someone else in interest is a lost opportunity for *you* to gain interest on that dollar. That's why lending/financing is such an important issue. When you lend to yourself or to others, you are instantly putting a natural law in motion that will begin to bring you a return. It's a natural byproduct of multiplication, and it's coming back to you and increasing at all times.

The question is, how do you put the powerful force of interest to work *for* you, instead of having it always work *against* you? And how do you begin to tap into this banking principle of increase if you don't own any "tier one" assets and have never been given a bank charter?

You begin by becoming your own banker.

KEY FINANCIAL PRINCIPLE: MAKE YOUR MONEY WORK FOR YOU, INSTEAD OF YOU CONTINUALLY WORKING FOR YOUR MONEY.

The Economic Destiny principles are timeless, tested, and effective for creating the outcomes you want for your financial security. Many of these time-tested principles and tools have been used in the banking industry for thousands of years.

As of this printing, the New York Stock Exchange (NYSE) has been around for 217 years, the 401(k) has been available as a financial tool for only about 35 years, while banking has stood the test of time for over 5,000 years.

What does a participating, cash-value, whole life policy from a mutual insurance company have to do with 5,000 years of banking principles? That is a very good question. Let's take a look at some of the practical applications many individuals are using today to become their own banker. You'll see some of the amazing benefits available for those who use these banking techniques.

THE POWER OF BECOMING YOUR OWN BANKER

"We spend more money on cars we drive *to work*,
than we ever mange *to save* in our retirement
accounts *at work!*" – Don Blanton

Consider this: How many cars have you purchased in the past 40 years? Or how many cars do you think the average person expects to purchase from age 28 to 58?

Assume you purchase a car every four years, and the average price of your car is $25,000. If you financed the car from a bank or credit union, your total payout in principal and interest would be approximately $29,000 (including depreciation), and you would be purchasing 10 cars over a 40-year span of time.

If you think this is an unusual scenario, it's not. But let's not get caught up on the number of cars purchased. Instead of cars, we could be discussing the amount you spend on credit cards, student loans, home loans, business loans, inventory, equipment, or vacations every four years. Yet cars provide a hypothetical that most people can relate to.

If you don't purchase that many cars, I'm sure you spend $6,250 every year on something, And $6,250 per year X 4 years = $25,000. OK, let's move on to the example and see what you're giving up by being someone else's customer instead of being your own banker.

You basically have four options when you purchase those cars:

• Option 1—You can *lease* them.

• Option 2—You can *finance* them from your credit union, bank or dealer.

- Option 3—You can *pay cash*, but few people have that kind of money in their savings account.

- Option 4—You can use the *IBC* plan (self-financing by using a properly structured whole life policy for privatized banking).

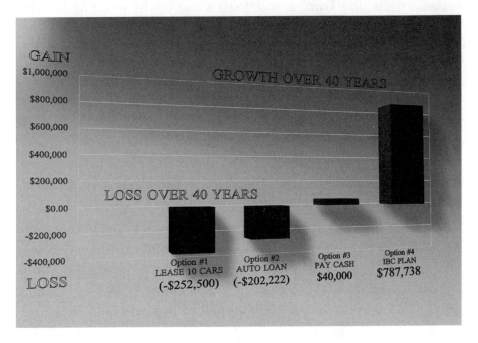

Notice that Option 4 (the *IBC* plan) recaptures your outgo and increases your wealth by $787,738 in total growth of your automotive dollars. How did that happen? Let me explain in detail.

If you choose Option 1 and lease the cars, your money flows out of your account and never returns back to you. Likewise, if you choose Option 2 and finance the cars, your principal and interest payments flow out of your account and never come back to you. So with either Option 1 or 2, your money is lost.

If you choose Option 3 and pay cash, you're not paying any interest to the lender, but your cash is tied up in the car. It has lost its power to continue to work for you. Since your cash has lost the opportunity to continue earning interest for you, you are paying a high "opportunity cost" for using your cash. Look at Option 3 on the graph again and see the real cost of your cash not earning interest for you over those 40 years.

If you choose Option 4, you are essentially borrowing the money from "The Bank of You." Like a good banker, you would always pay yourself back principal and interest payments during the 40-year term. Why? Because that's what you are currently doing with the banks and lenders. It's no different, except now *you own the bank!*

By the time you've paid yourself back the full amount you've borrowed from your own bank, you have already recaptured enough money to purchase your *next* vehicle, and you have recaptured any interest that's charged to you. Also, by choosing Option 4 (self-financing through *IBC*) over Option 3 (paying cash), you never expose yourself to paying an opportunity cost, because you are not losing the power of the cash working for you. When you choose Option 4, your money continues to earn interest and dividends on the full amount, because the cash stays in the insurance policy and keeps growing tax-free.

Imagine for a moment that you took $25,000 out of your savings account to buy the car. Would your bank or credit union still continue to pay you interest on that $25,000, even though the money has been withdrawn from your account? Of course not.

However, if you were to withdraw or borrow the $25,000 from your *IBC* policy, the money would still be working for you, earning interest income and dividends even though you have the money in your possession.

This concept may be hard to grasp at first, since the major banking and lending institutions are doing everything they can to push you toward ever-greater debt to *them*.

REVERSING YOUR CASHFLOW

You just witnessed the power of reversing the flow of your money back to yourself—just like the banks do. Although I gave you the example of a car purchase, imagine the possibilities if you did this with the money you use for vacations, college education, business inventory, missions projects, building expansions, or just about anything you might spend your money on. What if you could reverse the flow of your money, so that almost every dollar that flows *out* of your life is on a path to cycle back *into* your life?

Paying for things in cash is clearly much better than using debt and credit, and if you use cash you're well on your way to becoming a good steward of your resources. However, the INFINITE BANKING CONCEPT® has benefits that cash isn't able to offer. For example, without the *IBC* plan, you won't have the tax-free income advantages, and your money won't be working nearly as efficiently as it could.

ACTION STEP: FUND YOUR LONG-TERM INVESTMENT ACCOUNT WITH THE PRINCIPAL AND INTEREST PAYMENTS YOU SAVE.

If the last illustration seems to be going over your head or causing you to put up a wall because it has to do with insurance, you are not alone. There's a good reason for that feeling. I'm not covering this topic because I want you to go out and purchase whole life insurance tomorrow, but because this can be a powerful tool for implementing many of the long-term principles of the Economic Destiny Program.

As a good steward, you must find a safe place for your money to grow. You should make your decisions on time-tested principles and position yourself in low-risk investments that will steadily and predictably grow.

One of the best ways to do this is to learn how to become your own banker. The banking industry has been around for thousands of years, and bankers have skillfully mastered the process of making money grow in a variety of ways. The banking industry wants you to believe you are their *beneficiary*, when in fact, you most likely have been their *tool*.

The good news is that you can utilize the INFINITE BANKING CONCEPT to benefit from many of the same wealth-building tools the bankers have used for centuries. You can maximize and protect your investment dollars in ways you've never dreamed.

The key is to mimic the principles, systems and actions of those who are more successful than you are. By implementing your own virtual banking system, you can build a multigenerational surplus that is protected from taxes and the erosion of your principal contributions due to fees and market cycles.

By building a surplus, borrowing from yourself for all your financing needs, and then paying yourself back with interest, you not only profit from the interest payments, but you also recapture and retain your principal. Employing this strategy with the proper financial tool will change your economic destiny and teach you and your children the management techniques of a good and faithful steward. You'll be able to properly handle every dollar entrusted to your care.

What's your alternative? To remain a good customer of *someone else's* bank—building that bank's bright financial future while your family continues to struggle, wondering why they can't succeed in building wealth.

HOW THE BANKS DO IT

Banks succeed in creating and preserving wealth by focusing on three key principles we can learn from as well:

1. **BANKS FOCUS ON LENDING MONEY, NOT SPECULATIVELY INVESTING.** Lending generally creates predictable, contractual, guaranteed growth.

2. **BANKS TRANSFER RISK AWAY FROM THEMSELVES.** From this, we see the importance of being in total control of our money, instead of allowing someone else to be in control.

3. **BANKS TURN LIABILITIES INTO ASSETS.** They do this by earning more interest than they pay.

Expanding these three core banking principles, you can essentially become your own banker by taking a few simple steps and begin to:

- Turn wasted income into wealth that will last for generations.

- Fund your retirement plan.

- Eliminate debt quickly.

- Stop chasing rates of returns in unpredictable markets.

- Generate income that continues to flow into your life without having to work for someone else.

- Sleep better, knowing that your assets are growing instead of shrinking.

- Retire when you want to without losing your growth to penalties and taxes.

- Stop putting your money at risk and avoid loss and depreciation.

- Use a properly structured participating whole life policy form a mutual insurance company to gain access to your funds at any time, at any age, without having to qualify for a loan, and without paying any penalties or taxes.

If you mimic what banks and corporations have been doing for centuries, you can turn a lifetime of waste into generations of wealth. And if you *avoid* doing what the banks and lenders have been *telling* you to do for centuries, you will be taking a giant step toward becoming a wise steward of the resources entrusted to your care.

One wealth-building secret of banks and corporations is to minimize their taxes and maximize interest gains. You need to understand how they do this, so you can do the same.

Properly structured, participating cash-value whole life insurance from A-rated mutual insurance companies is an effective tool for reducing taxes and building wealth. Companies do this through Corporate Owned Life Insurance (COLI), and banks use Bank Owned Life Insurance (BOLI). But the same principles used by corporations and banks will work for individuals, businesses, churches, private schools etc, as well.

This program is an ideal alternative to speculative Wall Street investing. It is provided exclusively by mutual insurance companies that have excellent track records and are a much more stable place to put your money than a bank or the stock market. One reason for this stability is that mutual insurance companies are not highly leveraged like banks or retirement accounts. For every dollar mutual insurance companies lend out, they are required to have four dollars in reserves to back it up.

Banks, on the other hand, are leveraged the opposite way, usually 10 to 1. That means for every 10 dollars they lend out (your money), they are only required to hold one dollar on deposit in reserves. This is the exact opposite of the 1 to 4 ratio the mutual insurance companies are required to hold thus mutual insurance companies are the most stable pool of money in the world.

These insurance policies offer protection of your principal, contractually guaranteed interest payments, and annual dividends— all of which provide you with exponential growth of your cash value. Although the annual dividends are not guaranteed, the A-rated mutual companies have a consistent track record of paying out annual dividends every year, some for over 160 years. That means they haven't missed a single annual dividend payment—even during the Great Depression, two world wars, and the collapse of three major U.S. economic bubbles.

Here's a hypothetical example of what can be done with as little as a $420 per month contribution into a "properly structured" participating cash-value life insurance policy from a "mutual insurance" company:

Tom is 36 years of age and a nonsmoker. He contributes $420 per month to his plan. Day one after starting his plan, Tom has simultaneously accomplished two things. First, he has automatically created an instant estate of $190,000 to pass on to his family. Second, he has created cash value in his policy—yes, from day one.

In the first year, Tom has contributed $5,040 toward his policy, but he has instant access to $3,780 of his policy's cash value to use however he wishes (with no credit checks, penalties, or qualification requirements).

Now let's fast forward 10 years and look at the increase in value of Tom's estate. His estate (death benefit) increases in value every year, and after 10 years it has gone from $190,000 to $335,641.

Meanwhile, the cash value has also increased, from $3,503 to $55,978. At year 4½ , every penny Tom has paid into the policy is available to him in the cash value, so it's as if the insurance portion (death benefit) cost Tom nothing. The entire time, Tom has full access to his cash value—tax-free and penalty-free at any age. **REMEMBER:** Unlike with a 401(k), SEP, IRA or real estate equity, Tom has total control of his money at all times, and he will never have to pay capital gains taxes on the growth of his investment.[4]

Let's move forward to when Tom plans to retire, around the age of 70. Tom's death/estate benefit is now worth $726,850. Notice that the death/estate benefit increased by more than 100% from year 10 to year 30: from $335,641 to $726,850.

Tom's cash value has also increased, from $55,978 to an estimated $408,863 and he only contributed $170,000. Why? Because of unique features in the proper design of his policy, he is earning compound interest at an accelerated rate, and he earns tax-free dividends. Tom has a competitive contractually guaranteed interest rate of 4.50% for life on the cash value plus annual dividends, with a guarantee that no principal will be lost.[5]

Think about it: This remarkable financial tool enabled Tom's money to grow without the threat of the ups and downs of Wall Street or the real estate market. Best of all, his capital investment of only $170,000 from age 36 to 70 has built a tax-free estate worth over $1,135,713. Tom sleeps well at night and receives these benefits without putting his money at risk. And that's not all, it gets even better.

First, let's review....

---

4   Check with a privatized banking specialist to understand how this is accomplished
5   Guaranteed interest rates vary by company and designs of policy rate used is an example.

- Tom pays no taxes on the gains of his investment.

- He can draw on his cash value at any time as supplemental retirement income—tax-free and penalty-free, at any age.

- If he decides to stretch his retirement income out from age 70 to age 90, he can pay himself $24,532 every year for the next 20 years, and it's all tax-free. By age 70, Tom's estate is worth $726,850 in death benefits and $408,863 in cash value. His investment of only $170,000 from age 36 to 70 has built a tax-free estate worth over $1,135,713. If Tom passes away, he will be leaving a financial legacy for his family of over a million dollars, and not one penny of his wealth was taken from his family, because the death benefit passed on to his heirs free from income and estate taxes.[6]

Notice: By utilizing just the money Tom was wasting on car payments, he was able to create a million-dollar legacy for himself and his family!

This program works extremely well for the average individual. With guaranteed protection of principal, continuous growth of cash value, and access to tax-free capital when you need it, the benefits are truly amazing.

WHAT ABOUT TERM INSURANCE?

In the past, many financial gurus have recommended that people buy term life insurance instead of whole life. Because the premiums for term insurance are cheaper, these advisors would advise people to buy term and invest the difference in a long-term mutual fund account or something of that nature.

However, as time passed, it became clear that there was a major flaw in this approach: Most people who purchased term life insurance never invested the difference. As a result, their nest egg never grew, they were unable to withdraw funds, and the only way to receive any benefit from the policy was to *die*! If they did invest the differ-

---

6   Estate tax laws vary each year. In this example, the money did pass to his wife tax free. Example used for illustration purposes and is NOT intended as legal or tax advice. See your attorney or a legal tax consultant as appropriate.

ence what happened 97% of the time? To find out, read the Wise investor chapter again or watch the documentary "401(k) Meltdown" produced by the TV show 60 Minutes on CBS or CBS.com.

Term life insurance is not a financial tool. In essence, you are "renting" coverage—just in case you die before the term ends. The longer you have term insurance, the more expensive the rent becomes. Have you ever heard someone say "rent your house and invest the difference"? Of course not, that's absurd. A wise investor *owns* real-assets, they don't *rent* them. Term insurance is great for a short period of temporary "what if" coverage, but dying is not a "what if" event: It's a known fact that out of 1,000 people born, 1,000 people will die!

You do not want to base your life expectancy on an insurance agent's or an actuarial's terms, because only God knows when your time on earth will be up. Financial gurus also say things like, "Buy term insurance, and when you're rich at age 58 you can drop your coverage." But consider how absurd this advice is: You're paying for something you don't need for 20 years, and then you drop it right around the time you really begin to need it.

And while term insurance gets *more* expensive over time, whole life insurance gets *less* expensive over time. Don't just take my word for it—check out the facts.

WHAT YOU NEED TO KNOW

In 1993 Penn State University completed a study regarding term life insurance policies. The study examined over 20,000 term policies with an aggregate face amount of $4 billion. It included 1-5 year, 10 year, 20 year, and term to age to age 65 contracts which contained renewal and/or conversion features. Here are some interesting results of the study:

- More than 90% of all term policies are terminated or converted.

- 45% of all term policies are terminated or converted in the first year.

- 72% of all term policies are terminated or converted within the first three years.

- The average duration before termination or conversion is two years.

- Less than one policy in 10 survives the period for which it is written.

- After 15-20 years of exposure, less than 1% of all term life policies are still in force.

- Only 1% of all term insurance policies resulted in paying a death claim.

Consider the bottom line of the above findings: The odds are 100 to 1 *against* term insurance ever paying a death claim! Why would you want to pay money for a product that has such little chance of ever paying out a benefit?

The facts are undisputable:

- Less than 1% of term insurance policies ever pay out a death benefit to the insured's loved ones. In all likelihood, the premiums paid will simply be lost, with no benefit at all to the insured or his family. No wonder the premiums are cheaper!

Term life insurance does not accumulate cash value and has no contractual guarantee of growth. It offers none of the positive features of an IBC plan policy.

A properly structured participating cash-value whole life policy is actually a hybrid of both term and whole life insurance, so you get the best of both worlds—and so much more. These new policies offer a vast improvement over the past versions of participating cash-value whole life policies.

In the past, a typical whole life policy took years to build any cash value, but the insurance-based personal banking policy I'm revealing to you has cash value from day one. Please note: I'm *not* talking about a Universal Life policy or Variable Life policy. Those policies are tied to the market and are not designed for banking and do not line up with the time-tested principles taught in the Economic Destiny Program.

ACTION STEP: SET UP YOUR AUTOMATIC WEALTH-BUILDING ACCOUNT USING A PROPERLY STRUCTURED PARTICIPATING CASH-VALUE WHOLE LIFE POLICY FROM A MUTUAL COMPANY, CUSTOMIZED BY AN AGENT WHO'S A PRIVATIZED BANKING SPECIALIST WHO IMPLEMENTS THE STRATEGY IN THEIR OWN LIFE. YOU'LL FIND QUITE A DIFFERENCE BETWEEN SOMEONE WHO IS JUST OUT TO SELL YOU WHOLE LIFE INSURANCE AND AN AGENT WHO TRULY UNDERSTANDS THE BANKING PRINCIPLES I'M DESCRIBING.

This financial tool is a key component in creating your own family or business privatized banking system and taking control of your economic destiny. Look at how this perfectly fits in with the basic goals of the Economic Destiny Program:

- You gain control over your finances, becoming "the head and not the tail."

- You can borrow from yourself instead of becoming indebted to others. Car loans and even mortgages can be eliminated, since you have access to your own tax-free, penalty-free money.

- You can eliminate high interest payments, safely preserve your principal, and multiply your returns exponentially. As you make principal and interest payments back to yourself instead of to the bank, you begin to change the direction your money flows. Instead of always flowing away from you, your money now flows right back to you. This is what banks do to make their money grow exponentially, and by creating your own family banking system, you can learn to do it too.

A CASE STUDY

If you're still a little fuzzy on the *IBC* plan, that's OK. Here's a helpful case study to illustrate the benefits of how a participating whole life policy from a mutual insurance company can be used:

Table 1	Whole Life as a Savings Vehicle Starting with $3,131 a year premium (approximately $260 Per month)1			
Age of Insured	Net Premium	Cumulative Net Premium Outlay	Net Cash Value	Net Death Benefit
8	$3,131	$3,131	$1,712	$273,335
10	$3,131	$9,393	$6,767	$322,151
12	$3,131	$15,655	$12,824	$373,845
13	$3,131	$18,785	$16,507	$399,692
14	$3,131	$21,916	$20,410	$425,531
16	$3,131	$28,304	$29,110	$478,745
18	$3,131	$34,508	$38,923	$532,980
20	$3,131	$40,711	$49,849	$588,449
22	$3,131	$46,915	$62,217	$645,023
24	$3,131	$53,211	$76,340	$703,870
26	$3,131	$59,416	$92,228	$763,785
28	$3,131	$65,440	$109,893	$824,395
30	$3,131	$71,463	$129,802	$887,378
32	$3,131	$77,486	$152,315	$952,808
34	$3,131	$83,874	$178,101	$1,022,711
36	$3,131	$89,545	$206,412	$1,091,665
38	$3,131	$95,111	$238,232	$1,163,188
40	$3,131	$100,677	$274,168	$1,238,041
42	$3,131	$106,244	$314,750	$1,316,470
44	$3,131	$112,631	$361,355	$1,402,124
46	$3,131	$117,805	$412,584	$1,487,979
48	$3,131	$122,686	$469,858	$1,578,020
50	$3,131	$127,567	$533,963	$1,673,470
52	$3,131	$132,694	$605,848	$1,775,599
54	$3,131	$138,518	$686,680	$1,886,172
56	$3,131	$143,206	$775,489	$2,000,724
58	$3,131	$147,388	$873,586	$2,121,479
60	$3,131	$151,568	$982,562	$2,250,211
61	$3,131	$154,073	$1,041,922	$2,318,618
62	$3,131	$156,577	$1,104,442	$2,389,162
64	$3,131	$161,606	$1,239,770	$2,537,003
65	$3,131	$164,121	$1,312,850	$2,614,460

Policy Milestone: At age 16 the policy has capitolized The **"cash value"** now exceeds the amount of your premium contributions.

Policy Milestone: At age 28 the policy has reached a cash value of $109,893 but you have only paid $65,440 in premiums and the net death benefit increased to $824,395 and is growing larger each year.

Policy Milestone: At age 38 notice the total paid premium is only $95,111 but Your cash value is $238,232. Your child could take over the premium payments and his family is protected by $1,163,188 of death benefit.

Policy Milestone: Your net contribution has only been $117,805 in premiums but you now have $412,584 in cash value you can use as "tax free" retirement income. Also, notice that even when your paying yourself income your cash value continues to grow. Over the next 11 years the cash you used as retirement income is almost replaced. Isn't that powerful?

Polcy Milestone: Your son "the insured" is now retired and can draw off the $1,041,922 cash value "tax free". His family is also protected by the $2,318,618 in death benefit and you have left a legacy to the 1st, 2nd and 3rd generation.

Note: Table used with permission granted source Dwayne Burnell, MBA, author of *A Path to Financial Peace of Mind.* Table 1 is a hypothetical example and not a specific product for sale

In this case, Steve and his wife Linda want to have a multigenerational financial strategy that never puts their principal at risk. Their goal is to leave a financial legacy for several generations. They are primarily using this type of banking policy as a forced savings vehicle for the "living benefits," and the death benefit portion of the policy is only a secondary benefit.

Although Steve and Linda are the "owners" and "the beneficiaries" of the policy, their 8-year-old son is "the insured." Since Steve and Linda are the owners, they are the only ones with access to the cash value.

Your primary objective must be to maintain your principal while receiving consistent interest and dividend returns. During their investing years, Steve and Linda's money continued to grow and they never lost a penny of their principal—even when the markets were down and their friends were having a hard time sleeping.

Steve and Linda also had another benefit their friends did not have: When they finally retired and took money out of their account, they were able to spend every dime of it. Why? Because their *IBC* plan not only grew tax-deferred, but the income they drew from it was also free from income taxes and capital gains taxes.

Do you see how remarkable this outcome is? By using the *IBC* plan, you receive competitive returns without risking your principle—with little or no tax liability. Quite simply, it's been one of the best Wall Street alternatives for countless wise investors and that's why I'm now sharing this knowledge with you.

CASE STUDY 2

The following table illustrates a 50-year-old who wants to preserve his retirement nest egg, ensure that he won't run out of money in retirement, and leave a financial legacy to the next generation.

Remember Tom's results from the first case study? Not only did he recapture $408,863 in cash for his tax-free retirement income, but

Table 2	Whole Life as a supplemental income and wealth preservation strategy Starting with $50,000 a year premium for 5 years then dropping annual premiums down to 11,000 per year for 12 years then zero out of pocket premiums paid to the policy thereafter. (1)			
Age of Insured	Net Premium	Cumulative Net Premium Outlay	Net Cash Value	Net Death Benefit
48	$50,000	$50,000	$31,470	$1,054,411
49	$50,000	$100,000	$70,647	$1,150,511
50	$50,000	$150,000	$125,771	$1,246,677
51	$50,000	$200,000	$183,995	$1,343,247
52	$50,000	$250,000	$245,043	$1,453,805
53	$11,000	$261,000	$264,762	$1,430,768
54	$11,000	$272,000	$285,497	$1,423,709
55	$11,000	$283,000	$307,326	$1,418,797
56	$11,000	$294,000	$330,247	$1,415,962
57	$11,000	$305,000	$354,353	$1,415,256
58	$11,000	$316,000	$379,391	$1,415,918
59	$11,000	$327,000	$405,590	$1,417,937
60	$11,000	$338,000	$432,942	$1,421,228
61	$11,000	$349,000	$461,510	$1,428,005
62	$11,000	$360,000	$491,211	$1,432,266
63	$11,000	$371,000	$521,575	$1,439,252
64	$11,000	$382,000	$553,262	$1,448,262
65	$11,000	$393,000	$586,302	$1,459,182
66	$0	$393,000	$609,733	$1,471,887
67	$0	$393,000	$645,568	$1,486,127
68	$0	$393,000	$682,759	$1,501,504
69	$0	$393,000	$721,421	$1,518,188
70	$0	$393,000	$761,601	$1,535,887
71	$0	$393,000	$803,346	$1,554,901
72	$0	$393,000	$846,788	$1,575,384
73	$0	$393,000	$891,779	$1,597,665
74	$0	$393,000	$938,584	$1,621,889
75	$0	$393,000	$987,257	$1,647,901
76	$0	$393,000	$1,037,547	$1,675,304
77	$0	$393,000	$1,089,494	$1,704,044
78	$0	$393,000	$1,143,099	$1,734,304
79	$0	$393,000	$1,198,385	$1,766,299
80	$0	$393,000	$1,255,373	$1,800,273
81	$0	$393,000	$1,314,099	$1,836,195
82	$0	$393,000	$1,363,838	$1,874,573

Policy Milestone: Day one he deposited a $50,000 annual premium and created a $1,054,411 estate and from day one he has $31,470 in cash value at his disposal.

Policy Milestone: Year 6 the Policy is "capitalized" the "cash value is equal to his entire contributions up to that point.

Policy Milestone: At age 59 the cash value is $405,590 and the total premiums paid is only $327,000 and the death benefit is now $1,417,937 - notice the continuous growth.

Policy Milestone: At age 66 no more premiums are paid out of pocket - the $11,000 premium is being paid from policy values. the death benefit in this example is not decreasing in value because the annual dividends are larger than the annual premium. The policy is on auto pilot growth.

Policy Milestone: At age 73 only $393,000 was contributed to the policy, the cash value has grown to $891,779 and the death benefit is still growing. Do you see that the cost of this type of insurance is getting lower with age instead of higher?

Policy Milestone: At age 82 the cash value is $1,363,838. Remember that the cash value is accessible at any age, without penalty, and other benefits as described in this chapter. The death benefit has also continued to increase. When the insured dies any cash value that has been used and not paid back will be deducted from the death benefit amount before is passes to your heirs "TAX FREE" (3)

Note: Table 2 is another example showing how flexible and beneficial these policies can be. This is not an example of a specific product available for purchase.

he also built a legacy for his family and the next generation in the amount of $726,850. In all, Tom's estate grew to over $1,135,713. This would be impossible without the use of a properly designed policy. By using this financial tool for every major purchase, you allow your money to continually earn compound interest—24 hours a day, 7 days a week, 365 days per year.

In all the previous case studies, the policies were showing guaranteed growth, because they were designed to do just that, without putting any of the principal at risk. These illustrations show the incredible benefits even without using the INFINITE BANKING CONCEPT® strategy. But by maximizing the use of the policy for all major financing needs—instead of using the traditional methods of financing—the cash value and death benefit could exponentially multiply in size from the previous illustrations.

There's a reason why I didn't illustrate the maximization of benefits by applying the *IBC* plan here. One of those reasons is that the book you're now reading is not a sales tool—it's designed to expand your financial literacy. I want you to have a foundation of undisputed principles that will bring about an economic transformation in your life.

Perhaps at this point you realize that something you've been trained to do is simply not right. You might even see that most people support the conventional financial system—a system designed to keep them sick, in a position of lack, and in a posture of servitude. That is not your economic destiny!

Your economic destiny is to be transformed by the truth and prosper. I want to help set you free, not by my own wisdom, but by the truth.

SUGGESTED GUIDELINES

When it comes to financial investment options, one size does not fit all. However, I highly recommend that you work with someone who has implemented the Economic Destiny principles described in this book. Do your own research, and make sure to choose an advisor who displays a "you first" / "me second" mindset.

If you intend to contact an insurance professional to see if this type of program is compatible with your long-term wealth-building goals, please make sure they themselves are already practicing the *IBC* in their own lives and understand the INFINITE BANKING CONCEPT, inside and out. **REMEMBER:** This kind of insurance policy can be an extremely powerful tool, but it *MUST* be designed by someone with experience.

Most insurance professionals have never been trained on how to structure the proper policy for the *IBC* plan. You might even find that some insurance agents are resistant to offering you this kind of policy. Why? Because you have access to 65%, 75% or more of the cash value on day one, and this means the agents don't collect the big commissions they're accustomed to on the pure whole life policies they are trained to offer you.

Mutual insurance companies are not the same as publicly traded insurance companies like AIG—which were in the news during the 2008 economic meltdown. Mutual insurance companies are private and operate solely for the benefit of the individual policyholders. Publicly traded insurance companies have outside investors and shareholders to please, while Mutual Insurance companies do not.

In choosing the right mutual insurance company, you should look at its rating, longevity and ability to serve a customer's specific needs quickly and efficiently. When considering participating whole life as a financial tool, you must understand *what* you're buying and *why* you're buying it. Use good judgment, design a plan that meets your specific needs, and make sure it's the right thing for you.

The INFINITE BANKING CONCEPT® uses whole life insurance, but it's a lot different than your parents' or grandparents' insurance. Older designs of cash-value life insurance took years to build the cash value, because they were front-loaded with all kinds of fees and commissions. Today's participating cash-value life insurance builds accessible cash value quickly. In most cases, 67% to 70% of the money you've put in the policy is available to you when you open the policy, not months or years later.

The properly designed program with the right mutual insurance company uses design feature to maximize the growth of your cash value in the policy. This kind of tool simply wasn't available to your parents and grandparents. It's a professionally designed policy specifically created to enhance cash value growth and enable you to establish your family banking system as a full-circle financial tool.

CHOOSING AN INFINITE BANKING SPECIALIST

Not all insurance companies or agents are "created equal." Some have little or no experience in the kind of policy design requirements utilized by the INFINITE BANKING program.

If you have a conversation with an insurance agent about the possibility of using a participating whole life policy as a financial tool, you should ask him or her the following questions:

- Do they themselves use a participating whole life policy?

- Do they have participating whole life policies on their children?

- Are they using their whole life policies as financial tools, or just for death benefits?

- Are they able to speak clearly and specifically about the critical design elements that are necessary to craft a participating whole life "policy," usable as a wealth-building financial tool?

- Do they exhibit ease and knowledge in discussing the various aspects of your long-term financial goals?

- Are they discussing this approach with you as a lifelong strategy?

- Is the agent structuring the policy to meet your particular financial situation and provide the appropriate protection for you and your family?

If you have any doubts about the competence, knowledge or ethics of the insurance agent, STOP the process until you're confident you are getting the correct advice.

A FINAL COMMENT

If the policy is designed properly, participating whole life insurance is a powerful financial tool. But remember that this is essentially a two-part process:

1.   The policy must be designed and structured correctly in order to function optimally as a financial tool.

2.   You need an agent committed to helping you learn how to use its valuable features over the course of many years.

On the **www.youreconomicdestiny.org** website, you will find simple yet in-depth case studies on the subject of using participating whole life insurance as a waste-eliminating and wealth-building financial tool. The website will answer many of your questions and give you an opportunity to find an INFINITE BANKING CONCEPT specialist in your area.

In the next chapter, we're going to cover the most important and profitable investment of all: planting seeds in the lives of others. Of all the different types of investments you can make, this is the one that reaps the greatest rewards.

Chapter 15

SEEDTIME AND HARVEST
ECONOMIC DESTINY PRINCIPLE #7—
GIVING AND RECEIVING

"We make a living by what we get, but we make a life by what we give." —Winston Churchill

"You can have everything in life that you want if you will just help enough other people get what they want." —Zig Ziglar

GIVING OPENS UP THE WINDOWS OF HEAVEN. Our main purpose for building wealth is to position ourselves to be financial distribution centers for God. He not only provides us with the funds we need, but He also provides with opportunities to use those funds to be a blessing to others (Genesis 12:2).

In addition to making us stewards of the money we receive, God gives each of us abilities that He expects us to use wisely in serving His purposes on the earth. He has given me an ability to write and communicate effectively, and I have sought to use this precious gift to bring a message of hope and truth to bless the lives of others.

The principle of seedtime and harvest, giving and receiving, is woven into the fabric of everything God does. If we position ourselves to give away a portion of what God supplies us with, He will give us even more—and cycle continues

Before you can tap into the power of the 7th principle of the Economic Destiny Program—giving and receiving—you must understand how it operates. Giving is the most transformative principle in the Economic Destiny Program. If you want to receive the blessings and benefits promised to you in Deuteronomy 28, then it's paramount that you grasp this vital key for unlocking God's supernatural abundance.

KEY FINANCIAL PRINCIPLE: BEFORE YOU ARE ABLE TO GIVE, YOU MUST FIRST HAVE RECEIVED SOMETHING TO GIVE.

Giving and receiving is a natural law that God has put into motion. The very cycle of life gives us insights into the mechanics of how this principle operates.

You must have received something to give, before you'll be able to give—and you must keep giving in order to keep receiving.

A seed can't bear fruit by itself—it only contains the *potential* to bear fruit. Before a seed is able to transform into a harvest, it must be *planted*. As the seed grows, it begins to produce a harvest called fruit. From that fruit we receive nourishment, from nourishment we receive energy, and from energy we receive the strength to give of ourselves to others...and the cycle continues.

Giving and receiving mirrors the natural cycle of life. Those who choose to participate in this cycle will *inevitably* reap a harvest. However, when people choose to participate only in the *consumption* part of the cycle—failing to give back out of what they've received—they deny themselves the benefits of the cycle of giving and receiving, and eventually they wither and die.

Understanding the principle of giving and receiving will enable you to position yourself to become a powerful distribution center for the abundance God wants to give you. He blesses you so you in turn can BE a blessing to others (Genesis 12:2).

In our financial workshops, we sometimes hear people say, "Deep down in my heart, I really *want* to give, but I just don't have anything to give." But this is a misguided excuse. By the time you complete this chapter and fully understand the principle of giving and receiving, you will understand that you *already have* something of value to use in blessing others. If you are breathing, you've been receiving something of value that can be sown as a seed of blessing to those around you.

God not only has given you the gift of life, but He also has given you the ability to tap into an unlimited amount of His divine resources. You are the only one who can put limits on what you give. It's what you *choose* to do with what you've been given that will determine the harvest you receive back.

A FOUNDATION FOR GENEROUS GIVING

Everything I've shared in previous chapters has been a foundation for this Economic Destiny Principle about giving. We've discussed important principles such as planning, building a surplus, eliminating waste, reducing debt, and becoming a wise investor. Each of these principles has been an important seed of knowledge for transforming your economic destiny.

But until you grasp the importance of giving, something is still missing. In this chapter, you will learn how to plug into the giving and receiving cycle so you can continually receive overflowing resources and in turn be a blessing to your family and others.

KEY FINANCIAL PRINCIPLE: YOUR ULTIMATE FINANCIAL GOAL? POSITIONING YOURSELF TO ABUNDANTLY RECEIVE, SO YOU CAN ABUNDANTLY GIVE.

By positioning yourself to take action on this final principle of the Economic Destiny Program, you will help set in motion all the *other* financial laws as well. Giving is one of the most powerful principles outlined in the Bible, and it's a requirement for receiving increase in your personal financial circumstances. *Nothing* you freely give will return void—it cannot and it will not.

As you follow through on the first six steps of the Economic Destiny Program, you'll find that your personal needs are being met and you are creating a surplus in your savings and investment accounts. Your heart will begin to burn with a passion to share your blessings with your family and others.

THE LAW OF SEEDTIME AND HARVEST

There are spiritual guidelines for giving and receiving that anyone can use to impact their long-term financial success. Giving, planting seeds, reaping and investing are all components of this very important spiritual force.

God wants us to tap into His blessings and receive the outcomes promised in Deuteronomy 28. But one of the requirements for these blessings is to understand and implement the indispensable law of seedtime and harvest:

> While the earth remains,
> Seedtime and harvest,
> Cold and heat,
> Winter and summer,
> And day and night
> Shall not cease (Genesis 8:22).

Not only do we see this principle in nature, we also can see it at work all around us, in every area of our lives. Think about the businessman who puts money into a charitable foundation, to be given away to those in need. Though his motivation may have been to save on taxes, the more he gives, the more blessings come his way.

Or consider the venture capitalist who invests money into a new business with the expectation of receiving a return. We call this kind of investment *"seed* capital," and the investor is expecting a *harvest* from the seeds he sows.

The principle is clear: The more you invest in giving to others, the more you will receive in return. And the Bible says this law will be in effect as long as the earth remains.

DORIS BUFFET'S DISCOVERY

The story of Doris Buffet illustrates the reciprocal nature of the giving cycle—as your giving increases, so will your harvest of blessings:

Doris Buffet's mother positioned herself to be a financial blessing to her daughter. She diligently saved and invested, and in return reaped a harvest. She prepared herself to pass on a legacy to the next generation.

Doris was the recipient of her mother's harvest, and in return Doris has set a goal to pass the blessing along to others. So far, Doris has given away over $80 million to schools, charities, communities and organizations. Doris has set a goal to "die broke," and she's been quoted as saying, "I hope the last check I write will bounce!"

In the process of giving her blessings away, Doris has made an amazing discovery: The more she gives, the more God gives back to her. When Doris began her crusade of giving, she expected her bank account would continue to decrease until there was no more left to give. But to her dismay, she always discovered more money in her bank account than she had given away. Month after month, the increase she was receiving continued to out-pace her generous giving.

Doris says, "It's like being on a treadmill. The money keeps coming in faster than I can give it away!"

Doris has tapped into an endless supply of resources, because she is fully participating in the powerful cycle of giving and receiving, sowing and reaping. This is one of the purposes and benefits of having a surplus. It's not the amount of money Doris had to work with—it's what she **did** *with what she had that continued to bring the increase!*

The law of sowing and reaping isn't something that only works for a few select people. It's a universal Biblical principle that will work for *whoever* implements it:

> **Give, and it will be given to you: good measure, pressed down, shaken together, and running over will be put into your bosom. For with the same measure that you use, it will be measured back to you (Luke 6:38).**

> **It is more blessed to give than to receive (Acts 20:35).**

Please understand that giving is more than just an act of kindness that brings joy to the receiver. Giving sets a *spiritual law* into motion that blesses the giver. The apostle Paul described it this way:

> **He who sows sparingly will also reap sparingly, and he who sows bountifully will also reap bountifully...And God is able to make all grace abound toward you, that you, always having all sufficiency in all things, may have an abundance for every good work (2 Corinthians 9:6-8).**

SEEDS FOR YOUR FINANCIAL HARVEST

To change your current financial circumstances, it's crucial that you understand how to apply the Economic Destiny principle of giving and receiving, sowing and reaping. In order to consistently and faithfully give, you must first realize that you've already received something of value.

The law of sowing and reaping promises that if you sow a seed, you WILL reap a harvest:

> **Whatever a man sows, that he will also reap...And let us not grow weary while doing good, for in due season we shall reap if we do not lose heart (Galatians 6:7-9).**

Giving opens the door for opportunity. Many people have the mindset that they will begin giving to others *after* they receive a major financial breakthrough. As a result, they are always *waiting* before sowing seeds into the lives of others. They don't understand that giving and receiving are two sides of the same coin—on one side you give, and on the other side you receive. And to be able to give from one side, you must have already received on the other side.

Make no mistake about it: You already *have* something of value to give to others. How do I know? Because God "supplies seed to the sower," enabling everyone who has a willing heart to have something to give:

> Now may He who supplies seed to the sower, and bread for food, supply and multiply the seed you have *sown* and increase the fruits of your righteousness (2 Corinthians 9:10).

> If there is first a willing mind, it is accepted according to what one has, and not according to what he does not have (2 Corinthians 8:12).

RANDOM ACTS OF KINDNESS

KEY PRINCIPLE: THE GIFTS, TALENTS AND ABILITIES YOU HAVE ARE MEANT TO BE A BLESSING TO OTHERS.

After you begin to get your finances in order, look for opportunities to help someone else. Set aside a portion of your short-term savings specifically for that purpose.

To illustrate how the principle of giving can significantly impact the lives of others, let's look at Marilyn Mock's story:

Marilyn Mock of Rockwall, Texas, was prepared to find an investment opportunity in the wake of the 2008-2009 downturn in the real estate market. She had a surplus to invest and decided to go to an auction where some underpriced foreclosed homes were being sold. However, her investment turned out to involve a lot more than houses.

Marilyn was excited as she took her seat at the auction. She was about to make her first bid when she heard a little sniffle come from the woman beside her, whose name was Tracy. When Marilyn turned to ask her what was wrong, Tracy replied, "The home that is coming up next for auction is mine. I fell behind in a few payments after I lost my job, and I never could get caught up, so it's all being swept away."

Marilyn placed a bid on that home and won. After receiving confirmation of the winning bid, she turned to Tracy and said, "You no longer have to move. I just bought your house, and you can move back in tomorrow."

When Marilyn left home that day, she had no idea she would become such a blessing to a total stranger. Tracy had no idea that her prayers would be answered in such an unexpected and dramatic way.

Tracy said in a recent interview: "This act of kindness changed my life. Not only can I stay in my home, but the experience has returned my faith and hope to keep going and hold my head up. I know things happen for a reason."

Things sure do happen for a reason! Not only was Tracy blessed, but by faithfully putting herself into the middle of the giving cycle, Marilyn has had her blessing multiplied hundreds of times over. That one act of kindness changed her life forever, and it was the spark that gave her the idea of starting the Foreclosure Angel Foundation. She and the donors to her foundation are now helping thousands of homeowners like Tracy, who are in jeopardy of losing their homes. This all happened because she was prompted to participate in the giving cycle.

Usually you don't have to look very far for an opportunity to give. Just open your heart and listen to the still, small voice of God's Spirit, and you will find the perfect opportunity to get started. You can begin making a difference in someone's life *today* by planting a seed into Marilyn's charitable foundation: **WWW.FORCLOSUREANGLEFOUNDATION.COM.**

GIVING DESPITE LEAN TIMES

Perhaps you're going through tough times right now, and your only focus has been on getting your own finances on track. I understand. I've been through lean financial times too.

But no matter what your present situation may be, you can transform your financial destiny by planting seeds in the lives of others. Your objective is to become an overflowing distribution center, and this often begins with one act of kindness toward another. Many people have found that their financial turnaround started when they sacrificially helped someone else during their own lean times.

For example, the Bible tells the story of a widow who was so poor that she only had enough food for one more meal for her and her son. Despite her dire circumstances, the prophet Elijah asked her to feed *him* first. Amazingly, when the woman did so, she tapped into God's giving cycle: "She and her household ate for many days. The bin of flour was not used up, nor did the jar of oil run dry" (1 Kings 17:15-16).

Another Biblical passage describes how Isaac sowed seeds in a time of *famine* (Genesis 26:1). That must have been quite a step of faith, because the natural reaction to lean times is to *hoard* our seeds instead of sow them. Yet we're told that "Isaac *sowed* in that land, and *reaped* in the same year a hundredfold; and **the LORD blessed him**. The man began to prosper, and continued prospering until he became **very prosperous** (Genesis 26:12-13). God abundantly blessed Isaac's sowing!

GOD THE GIVER

Giving brings encouragement and hope to both the receiver and the giver. Solomon tells us, "The generous will prosper; those who refresh others will themselves be refreshed" (Proverbs 11:25 NLT).

By His very nature, God is a Giver (John 3:16). Since He is a generous God, He wants His people to be generous too! He not only wants us to have everything we need, but He also wants us to have enough to share with others:

God loves a cheerful giver, and God will provide all you need, **plenty left over to share with others**. "They share freely and give generously to the poor. Their good deeds will be remembered forever" (2 Corinthians 9:7-9 NLT).

ACTION STEP: LOOK FOR OPPORTUNITIES TO HELP SOMEONE ELSE.

Make it a priority to plant seeds of knowledge in your children, teaching them how to properly manage money. Then take the next step and help someone else get their financial house in order. Make it your goal to share these principles with at least five other families in need. Give them a copy of this book, point them to the resources at www.youreconomicdestiny.org, or start a small group or class where you can teach these principles on a regular basis.

ACTION STEP: ONCE YOU HAVE LEARNED THE PRINCIPLES OF THE ECONOMIC DESTINY PROGRAM, BECOME A FINANCIAL MENTOR TO OTHERS. SET UP WORKSHOPS IN YOUR LOCAL CHURCH OR COMMUNITY TO TEACH PEOPLE WHO WANT TO BECOME FINANCIALLY INDEPENDENT.

There are people all around you who are in need of encouragement and hope. Take a few minutes to consider whether you know someone who needs to be touched by your generosity—a neighbor, a family member, a coworker, someone at church, the school bus driver, your children's teacher?

ANONYMOUS GIVING

Maybe you've held back in the past for fear of rejection, not wanting the recipient to feel embarrassed or worry that strings might be attached to the gift. If there are reasons it would be awkward to give them a gift directly, you might want to find a way to touch their lives anonymously.

Misha and Lionel Thompson, a mother and father from Bellingham, Washington, went through a season of financial setbacks. But during their economic storm neighbors provided an unexpected outpouring of generosity. The kindness they received made a lasting impression on the Thompsons.

Misha remembers her feelings while standing at the doorstep accepting groceries from friends and neighbors. Although grateful for the blessings, she remembered the awkwardness, and she determined that she never wanted another mother in need to experience those feelings. But Misha knew that when she made it through her difficult season, she was going to do something to give back!

She and her husband created a nonprofit organization where givers can give anonymously to anyone, anytime, without creating those awkward feelings of embarrassment or strings attached. The receiver has the opportunity to call and leave a thank you voice message that's delivered to the giver via an e-mail voice file.

Think about the amazing opportunity Misha and Lionel provided to givers: People can plug into the giving cycle and give to whomever they want, whenever they want. They could be supporting a family or an entire neighborhood that needs to be touched by your blessings—and they will never know who to give thanks to, except God!

This anonymous giving process is the mirror image of Christ's teaching in Mathew 6:3-4. Jesus instructs us exactly how we should provide charity to those in need, and He lets us know how we will receive our reward if we give in this way: "When you do a charitable deed, do not let your left hand know what your right hand is doing, that your charitable deed may be in secret; and your Father who sees in secret will Himself reward you openly."

Imagine being used to anonymously send a blessing to someone in need, and the recipient feeling blessed directly from the hand of God. If God has put someone on your heart, you can plant a seed and begin reaping a harvest at Giving Anonymously: www.givinganon.org.

THE REAL AMERICAN DREAM

America is one of the most generous nations on earth. Did that happen just because of the abundant amount of resources we've been blessed with? Or did our overflowing blessings come from the fact that we first were givers? According to the principle of giving, it must be the latter.

The *real* American Dream is not about having the most material assets, but rather it's about managing the resources you're blessed with in order to be a blessing to others. Yes, this is the land of opportunity, but what you *do* with those opportunities will determine what kind of legacy you will leave.

In order to leave a financial legacy, it's crucial to have a plan in place to accomplish two primary objectives:

- Taking financial care of your family in case something unexpected happens to you during your working years
- Leaving wealth through your estate to loved ones or charities

Of course, the *best* legacy you can give your children is knowledge of God's Word. Also, teach them how to manage money. This kind of training in Biblical precepts ideally should start at an early age:

Train up a child in the way he should go, And when he is old he will not depart from it (Proverbs 22:6).

With a proper foundation of Biblical knowledge and sound financial economics, your children will have a great opportunity for financial success.

This Book of the Law shall not depart from your mouth, but you shall meditate in it day and night, that you may observe to do according to all that is written in it. For then you will make your way prosperous, and then you will have good success (Joshua 1:8).

The goal for your children is not for them to remain dependent upon you for their financial resources, but for them to prosper because they are implementing God's principles in their own life.

MULTIGENERATIONAL BLESSINGS

Many are content to live paycheck to paycheck, happy to have enough just to pay their monthly bills. Others have planned for their retirement, consistently saving and investing funds that will eventually grow into a sizeable retirement account for their senior years. But shouldn't it also be a priority to create a financial reserve that will bless our children and grandchildren?

Solomon offers us an insight on this: "A good man leaves an inheritance to his children's children" (Proverbs 13:22). A "good man," in this context, is someone who prepares well, having a vision and action plan for blessing future generations. Such a person wants to send blessings to generations they may never see.

God can see the future, and He knows the needs of your great great grandchildren! Even though you may never meet them, He can use your financial legacy as a blessing in their lives.

God would not have given us His divine wisdom to plan our financial affairs beyond our own generation if it were not part of His plan for us to do so. He's interested in our prosperity *and* in the prosperity of our descendants!

Not only did God tell Abraham that He would bless him in order to make him a blessing to others (Genesis 12:2-3), but he also promised repeatedly that these same blessings would come upon Abraham's *descendants* (e.g., see Genesis 12:7, 13:15, 15:13-14, 15:18, 16:10, 17:7-9). Not only that, but God also told Abraham he would receive blessings of faith and finances so enormous that "in you all the families of the earth shall be blessed" (Genesis 12:3). *What an incredible legacy!*

MOTIVATED BY LOVE

Your motivation for building wealth and leaving a legacy for future generations must not be for a personal reward or acclamation. Your motive must be LOVE, and your legacy is a byproduct of that love. God is concerned with your *heart* first, not the size of your wallet or the inheritance you leave.

If your heart is right with God, your motives will be right, and you will be following Biblical principles for managing your resources. You will be a powerful instrument for distributing a financial legacy to future generations.

ACTION STEP: ESTABLISH A PLAN FOR YOUR FAMILY'S FINANCIAL LEGACY.

Teach your children financial responsibility while they are young and while you are still with them. Help them develop good financial management skills. Visit **www.youreconomicdestiny.org** to see a list of tips for teaching your children sound financial skills.

ACTION STEP: DEVELOP A PLAN TO TEACH YOUR CHILDREN ABOUT SOUND FINANCIAL PRINCIPLES. AND REMEMBER: YOUR CHILDREN WILL BE MORE IMPACTED BY THE EXAMPLE YOU SET THAN BY WHAT YOU TELL THEM!

SEEDS OTHER THAN MONEY

Money certainly isn't the only seed that will produce a financial harvest. Your time, talents and experiences are valuable assets you already have. Many people are overlooking assets and gifts like these, which often are keys for producing additional income.

Perhaps you're not yet where you want to be financially, and maybe you think your current income is simply too low to cover your living expenses. If so, first make sure you are following the Economic Destiny steps to live within your means. Then start planting seeds to increase the amount of your income.

Listed below are some practical suggestions for increasing your income, based on assets and gifts you already have:

1. **SOW SEEDS FOR A BETTER JOB.** Take an inventory of your current skills. Prepare a resume and cover letter that clearly describe how your skills will add value to a business or organization.

ACTION STEP: IDENTIFY FIVE INDIVIDUALS OR COMPANIES WHERE YOU WILL SEND YOUR COVER LETTER AND RESUME IN PURSUIT OF A JOB THAT PROVIDES MORE INCOME.

2. **INCREASE YOUR KNOWLEDGE BASE.** Spend time increasing your knowledge, experience and marketable skills. You can become better educated in any field over a 12 to18-month period. Invest time reading relevant books, doing research on the Internet, or talking to experts in that field.

ACTION STEP: MAKE A LIST OF PRACTICAL STEPS TO INCREASE YOUR KNOWLEDGE AND SKILLS IN ORDER TO BECOME MORE VALUABLE IN YOUR PRESENT JOB OR BUSINESS.

3. **VOLUNTEER YOUR SERVICES.** Select local charities, businesses, agencies, or ministries that are providing service in an area that interests you. Find ways your skills and experiences can be of benefit, and then volunteer your time. Volunteer work can be a seed of time that rebounds into your life with added blessings, new experiences, and valuable networking opportunities.

ACTION STEP: LIST FIVE INDIVIDUALS OR FAMILIES THAT WOULD BENEFIT FROM LEARNING THE ECONOMIC DESTINY PRINCIPLES FOR GETTING OUT OF DEBT AND BUILDING LONG-TERM WEALTH. THERE ARE MANY PEOPLE IN YOUR AREA WHO NEED THIS TYPE OF FINANCIAL MENTORING.

4. **GIVE AWAY YOUR KNOWLEDGE TO THE POOR.** Those who live in poverty often need a financial education far more than they need a handout. Select a family in financial need, and start planting seeds of economic knowledge into their lives. Let them know that God loves them and wants them to have a friend and mentor to share the tools they will need to prosper.

ACTION STEP: PLANT A SEED OF YOUR TIME WITH A NEEDY FAMILY TO HELP THEM GET THEIR FINANCES IN ORDER.

By implementing the practical steps above, you will set in motion the law of giving and receiving. Get ready to be blessed!

You can transform your own financial destiny and the destiny of your descendants by using your unique gifts, talents and abilities. Don't wait for a financial windfall in order to get started, for you already have something of value to bless others.

REMEMBER: *The gifts and assets you have may be the answer to someone else's prayer.*

ACTION STEP:

VISIT WWW.YOURECONOMICDESTINY.ORG TODAY AND ENROLL IN THE "YOUR ECONOMIC DESTINY" MENTORING PROGRAM. YOUR LIFE WILL NEVER BE THE SAME!

While at the website be sure to visit the "Field of Dreams", where you will see lives are being changed daily by the seeds other readers have already planted.

In the next chapter, you'll learn how to turbo-charge your financial increase by applying the most important tool of all—"faith"—to your finances.

Chapter 16
FAITH AND YOUR FINANCES
THE KEY TO WALKING IN ABUNDANCE

"Through persistence, self-knowledge, prayer, commitment, optimism, a resolute trust in God and the building of your own personal moral strength, you can enjoy the blessings of a deeper faith and face the difficulties of life with courage and confidence."
—Norman Vincent Peale

"Now faith is the substance of things hoped for, the evidence of things not seen." —Hebrews 11:1

A S A FINANCIAL COACH, I find many people who are frustrated with their current financial situation and fearful of economic conditions in the future. There clearly seems to be a spiritual dimension to all of this.

Once you have learned the principles of the Economic Destiny Program, it's important to understand the role faith plays in your long-term financial success. Faith is the key ingredient in fulfilling God's purpose and destiny for your life. With a clear vision and a well-designed plan executed in faith, *anyone* can transform their existing circumstances and walk in the economic inheritance God has promised—regardless of the economic circumstances around them.

This is not just a theoretical issue for me. I speak from personal experience. The story of my own life illustrates how faith can transform a person's financial circumstances, taking them from despair to hope.

As you glean from my personal story at the beginning of this book, I learned a very important lesson that will stay with me for the rest of my life:

GOD ANSWERS PRAYER! THROUGH FAITH, HE CAN—AND DOES—INTERVENE IN PEOPLE'S CIRCUMSTANCES.

The lessons I learned from my own experiences have deeply impacted the direction of my life, and I'm confident they can do the same for you. Biblical principles such as faith, hope, and charity are able to transform an individual, a family, a community or a nation.

APPLYING THE LESSON

God has put within every individual gifts, talents and abilities to live a life of purpose and destiny. There are no valid excuses, for He has provided us with everything we need to live a successful and productive life (2 Peter 1:3).

However, many people never fulfill their God-given purpose, and often this is because they've allowed themselves to be enslaved by their financial circumstances. Instead of seeing and tapping into God's provision, they focus on what they don't have.

This mindset of focusing on your lack instead of God's provision will hold you back from the victory that is already within your reach. You must be confident enough in God's promises to *know* your victory exists. Regardless, of your present circumstances, you must see your eventual victory through the eyes of faith, expecting God to give you success.

Consider the Olympic athletes who practice hard with rigorous daily training. They don't make these sacrifices with an expectation of failing! No, they continually see victory before them, even though it does not yet exist.

Faith and expectancy are two critical elements that work together synergistically to produce our success:

1. Faith is characterized by expectancy.

2. Faith and expectancy work together to motivate us toward the actions we must take to achieve the outcomes we envision.

REMEMBER: Our attitudes and mindsets play a very important role in the actions we take. When faith includes both expectancy and corresponding action, it enables us to overcome current limitations and negative circumstances. In that way, faith becomes a powerful force for achieving our goals, in our finances or any other part of our lives.

ACTION STEP: TAKE A STEP OF FAITH, AND MOVE IN THE DIRECTION OF YOUR DESIRE. AS YOU EXERCISE YOUR "FAITH MUSCLE," YOUR ACTIONS WILL FOLLOW WHAT YOU BELIEVE. REMEMBER: YOU MUST BELIEVE THAT GOD WILL ACT ON YOUR BEHALF IF YOU FOLLOW HIS INSTRUCTIONS.

RECEIVING GOD'S ABUNDANCE

"Faith by itself, if it does not have works, is dead. But someone will say,

'You have faith, and I have works.' Show me your faith without your works, and I will show you my faith by my works." —James 2:17-18

Faith is the driving force behind most human success stories. One of the most important keys to walking in God's abundance is to understand that He wants you to be successful and has already made provisions for your success.

Conrad Hilton once observed, "Success...seems to be connected with action. Successful men and women keep moving. They make mistakes, but they don't quit." Faith understands that your existing circumstances can be overcome if you access God's abundance in order to fulfill His purpose and destiny for your life. Through the law of faith, you can supersede all past mistakes and current financial circumstances.

But in the economic arena or any other part of your life, your faith must be established by your actions. James 2:26 states that "faith without works is dead." In order to receive the blessings God promises to people of faith, you must ensure that your *actions* line up with your *beliefs*.

According to Deuteronomy 28:2, God's financial blessings are automatic for those who are obedient to His principles. Yet notice that it's not enough to "claim God's promises"—you must act on the principles in His Word.

> **KEY FINANCIAL PRINCIPLE:** TO ACHIEVE SUCCESS AND FULFILL YOUR DESTINY, YOU MUST SEEK GOD'S WISDOM AND FOLLOW HIS INSTRUCTIONS. ALL THE RESOURCES YOU NEED TO CHANGE YOUR CIRCUMSTANCES ALREADY EXIST IN THE INVISIBLE WORLD OF FAITH. ALL THAT'S NEEDED IS THE WISDOM TO TRANSFER IT INTO THE NATURAL WORLD.

LIMITLESS RESOURCES

God's provisions are limitless. There is no dream too big for Him to bring to reality, no dismal financial circumstances too difficult for Him to change. "I am the LORD, the God of all mankind," He tells us, "Is anything too hard for me?" (Jeremiah 32:27) But in order to walk in His abundance, you must have faith in His promises and be a good steward over what you already have.

Joseph was a perfect example of how this principle operates. In Genesis 39, Joseph was wrongfully imprisoned and held captive by circumstances beyond his control. Yet all that changed in a moment of time:

Pharaoh said to Joseph, "See, I have set you over all the land of Egypt." Then Pharaoh took his signet ring off his hand and put it on Joseph's hand; and he clothed him in garments of fine linen and put a gold chain around his neck. And he had him ride in the second chariot which he had; and they cried out before him, "Bow the knee!"

So he set [Joseph] over all the land of Egypt. Pharaoh also said to Joseph, "I am Pharaoh, and without your consent no man may lift his hand or foot in all the land of Egypt" (Genesis 41:41-44).

Joseph had *nothing* when he was taken captive and brought to Egypt. But by being faithful with the gifts God had given him, he eventually was promoted to a position of awesome authority. His faithfulness not only changed his own circumstances, but it also changed the economic destiny of an entire nation. By maintaining a good attitude and remaining faithful, he proved that God and people could trust him. As unlikely as it seemed at the time, God fulfilled the dreams He had given Joseph many years earlier.

If you are not faithful with what you have, you won't be faithful if given more (Luke 16:10-12). God is an incredibly generous Heavenly Father, but His full abundance is reserved for those who are faithful with the resources He's already entrusted to their care.

ACTION STEP: TAKE AN INVENTORY OF THE RESOURCES YOU ALREADY HAVE. YOUR BREAKTHROUGH IS DEPENDENT ON WHAT YOU CURRENTLY HAVE, NOT WHAT YOU WILL RECEIVE IN THE FUTURE. GOD HAS ALREADY PROVIDED YOU WITH THE TIME, GIFTS, SKILLS AND CONTACTS YOU MUST PLANT AS SEEDS IN ORDER TO RECEIVE AN INCREASE.

As stewards, we must learn to follow God's instructions and not waste His resources. We must learn the true purpose of wealth and be willing to be God's coworker in blessing others as we release His blessings on the earth.

Yes, God still answers prayer, and He gives true wealth to those who prepare themselves. As in Joseph's case, the Lord can bring a quick turnaround to those who prove faithful. One day Joseph was in prison, with little hope for a change in his circumstances. But the next day he was prime minister of the most powerful nation in the world.

REMEMBER: God wants us to enjoy the benefit of the resources He's entrusted to us. However, instead of consuming everything on ourselves, He wants us to use our gifts, talents and abilities to be bless others.

FAITH FOR A FINANCIAL TURNAROUND

If you are in a financial pit today, you're not alone. At the time this book is being written, an estimated one out of every four homeowners is "under water," owing more on their mortgage than the house is worth in today's market.

David and many other Biblical writers testified that God is willing and able to bring His people out of the pits they get themselves into:

I waited patiently for the LORD;
And He inclined to me,
And heard my cry.
He also brought me up out of a horrible pit,
Out of the miry clay,
And set my feet upon a rock,
And established my steps.
He has put a new song in my mouth—
Praise to our God;
Many will see it and fear,
And will trust in the LORD.
Blessed is that man who makes the LORD his trust (Psalm 40:1-4).

No financial situation is too difficult for those who have faith. God is still in control, and He shows His favor to those who trust in Him and act upon His instructions. In His Word, He provides abundant wisdom and practical advice about money and success. Through the prayer of faith, He provides access to His provisions and miraculously intervenes in our circumstances.

ACTION STEP: IN ORDER TO RECEIVE YOUR DESIRED FINANCIAL OUTCOMES, EXPAND YOUR VISION AND INCREASE YOUR FAITH. HEBREWS 11:1 SAYS, "NOW FAITH IS THE SUBSTANCE OF THINGS HOPED FOR, THE EVIDENCE OF THINGS NOT SEEN."

REMEMBER: Your faith cannot be separated from your actions. The principle of stewardship must be clearly understood and thoroughly mastered in order to fully walk in God's abundance.

As pointed out concerning the Parable of the Talents in an earlier chapter, money was taken from the poor manager and given to the one who managed his money properly (Matthew 25:26-28). The choices you make and actions you take are critical to fulfilling God purpose and destiny for your life.

Are you praying for a financial windfall? That's wonderful, but if God blesses you with a financial miracle, it will quickly disappear if you have not learned how to manage it. The Bible warns those who don't follow God's stewardship principles: "In the blink of an eye wealth disappears, for it will sprout wings and fly away like an eagle" (Proverbs 23:5 NLT).

ACTION STEP: FOLLOW THE LORD'S INSTRUCTIONS IN EXPECTATION OF RECEIVING HIS PROVISION. INSTEAD OF EXPECTING LACK, YOU MUST EXPECT ABUNDANCE AND TAKE ACTION TO PREPARE FOR THAT DESIRED OUTCOME.

OVERCOMING FINANCIAL FRUSTRATION

"We seem to gain wisdom more readily through our failures than through our successes. We always think of failure as the antithesis of success, but it isn't. Success often lies on just the other side of failure." —Leo F. Buscaglia

There are many reasons people may find themselves frustrated by their financial circumstances. Often they're in a financial pit because of mistakes they've made, but at other times, they're suffering from circumstances beyond their control.

I've met many people who have a dream for a business or ministry that requires finances they simply don't have. They need a financial breakthrough if their dreams are ever to be fulfilled.

The good news is this: God is a God of turnarounds! Solomon explains: "Unrelenting disappointment leaves you heartsick, but a sudden good break can turn life around" (Proverbs 13:12 The Message).

But in order to get "a sudden good break" or turnaround, we must be serious about seeking God and obeying His Word: "When you get **serious** about finding Me and want it more than anything else, I'll make sure you won't be disappointed...I'll turn things around for you" (Jeremiah 29:13-14 The Message).

The Scriptures also remind us that we may need patience in order to receive our financial breakthrough: "Do not become sluggish but imitate those who through *faith* and *patience* inherit the promise" (Hebrews 6:12). But although patience may be needed, we can be confident of this: When God gives us a *vision*, He will also give us the *pro-vision*.

For believers, the *ultimate* turnaround will come when we receive TOTAL abundance in our heavenly home: "The time is coming when I will turn EVERYTHING around for My people!" (Jeremiah 30:3) But we don't need to wait until then. Even in this life, our Heavenly Father wants to meet our needs and show us His overflowing provision.

GOD'S INTERVENTION

Perhaps you are in such a financial pit that it's hard to even imagine what your financial turnaround could look like. Yet look at these amazing Biblical examples of God's intervention in people's circumstances:

- **DAVID:** In the morning he was merely a shepherd boy, but by that afternoon he had become a national hero (1 Samuel 17).

- **JOSEPH:** One day he was in prison, and the next day he was prime minister of the most powerful nation in the world (Genesis 41).

- **DANIEL:** One day he was in desperate circumstances—in captivity and thrown into a lion's den. The next day he was reinstated to a high government position (Daniel 6).

- **A POOR WIDOW:** At the beginning of the day, she and her son were expecting to eat their last meal and die, but by the end of the day she had an abundant supply of food (1 Kings 17:12-16).

- **GIDEON:** One day he was fearfully threshing grain at the threshing floor. The next day he was the leader of an army that would bring deliverance to his people (Judges 6 & 7).

Of course, God's intervention is not always as dramatic as in these examples. Just because you plant seeds of some kind today, it doesn't necessarily mean your harvest will appear within 24 hours. (We really *do* live in a microwave, drive-through, ATM machine society, don't we?)

Whatever your circumstances may be, trust God and sow seeds in faith, waiting for your provision to come. If you follow God's principles, you can be *certain* your breakthrough WILL come!

If your current situation seems hopeless, take steps to get your financial house in order. God wants to give you His supernatural provision, but He will supply the *"super"* only after you trust Him and supply the *"natural."*

Once you're practicing the principles of good stewardship, the next step is to use your faith to generate additional revenue. If you are not happy with your current income, it's time to ask God for creative ideas to utilize your talents and gifts. Ask Him to show you ways to make yourself more valuable to your present employer or in the wider marketplace.

God will inspire you to use your talents and gifts you already have to produce more income than you can presently imagine. Identify a need in someone else's life, and become a solution to that person's problem. The bigger the problem, the bigger your compensation is likely to be when God enables you to solve it.

ACTIONS CORRESPONDING TO YOUR FAITH

To find lasting success in the financial arena, you must believe what God says in His Word, and then *act upon* what you believe. If you are caught in circumstances that prevent you from completing your assignment from God, then change your actions.

Use your faith and take action to reposition yourself to do what God has instructed you to do. As part of His financial plan for your life, recognize that there are important priorities to consider as you seek to put your faith into action.

ACTION STEP: FOCUS YOUR FAITH ON WHAT GOD HAS PROMISED, AND REPOSITION YOUR LIFESTYLE ACCORDINGLY.

Notice the boldness with which Jesus encourages us to believe and act:

> **For assuredly, I say to you, whoever says to this mountain, "Be removed and be cast into the sea," and does not doubt in his heart, but believes that those things he says will be done, he will have whatever he says. Therefore I say to you, whatever things you ask when you pray, believe that you receive them, and you will have them (Mark 11:23-24).**

This brief passage is full of powerful concepts. For example, Jesus says His promise is not just for a select few, but rather for **"whoever"** believes and acts in faith. YOU can be part of that "whoever"!

Jesus also makes it clear that we should pray BIG prayers, for we can have **"whatever"** we ask! What a great faith-building promise: *Whoever* can have *whatever*!

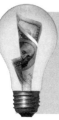

ACTION STEP: REALIZE THAT GOD HAS THE POWER AND DESIRE TO INTERVENE ON YOUR BEHALF. HE CAN INTERVENE AND TRANSFORM HOPELESS FINANCIAL CONDITIONS INTO ABUNDANCE.

Over the centuries, the time-tested principles discussed in this book have changed the lives and destinies of countless thousands who dared to put the precepts to the test. But remember that knowledge alone will never get the job done. You must be willing to take the action steps necessary and apply God's financial principles to your life. Act on what you have learned, stir your faith into action, and watch God's promises come to pass.

ACTION STEP: COME TO GOD IN FAITH, ASKING HIM TO SHOW YOU HOW TO USE THE GIFTS AND TALENTS YOU ALREADY HAVE TO CREATE ABUNDANCE. HE CAN CHANGE YOUR CIRCUMSTANCES, BUT YOU MUST BE WILLING TO ASK AND ACT.

SCRIPTURES FOR FINANCIAL INCREASE

Listed below are some powerful scriptures taken directly from the Word of God regarding your economic destiny. Take time to meditate on these verses daily. Put them on 3x5 cards and speak them out loud throughout the day.

Declare them as true and they will activate your faith. You'll find yourself able to overcome negative financial situations and walk in God's abundance.

These scripture passages will also help you focus your actions on the steps you must take to see God's promises fulfilled in your life. You will begin to see His power and provision transform your financial circumstances.

I DECLARE:

- This Book of the Law shall not depart from my mouth, but I shall meditate in it day and night, that I may observe to do according to all that is written in it. For then I will make my way prosperous, and then I will have good success (Joshua 1:8).

- I will seek first the kingdom of God and His righteousness, and all these things shall be added to me (Matthew 6:33).

- I shall remember the LORD my God, for it is He who gives me power to get wealth, that He may establish His covenant (Deuteronomy 8:18).

- The Lord desires above all things that I may prosper and be in health, even as my soul prospers (3 John 2).

- The Lord has pleasure in my prosperity, for I am His servant (Psalm 35:27).

- My God shall supply all my needs according to His riches in glory by Christ Jesus (Philippians 4:19).

- The LORD will open to me His good treasure, the heavens, to give the rain to my land in its season, and to bless all the work of my hand. I shall lend to many nations, but I shall not borrow. And the LORD will make me the head and not the tail; I shall be above only, and not be beneath, for I will heed the commandments of the LORD my God and be careful to observe them (Deuteronomy 28:12-13).

- The Lord, my God, teaches me to profit, and leads me by the way that I should go (Isaiah 48:17).

- Because I seek the Lord, I shall not lack any good thing (Psalm 34:10).

- He who spared not His own Son, but delivered Him up for us all, shall also freely give me all the things that I need (Romans 8:32).

- Christ has redeemed me from the curse of the law, being made a curse for me…that the blessing of Abraham might come upon me (Galatians 3:13-14).

- God will go before me and make the crooked places straight: He will break in pieces the gates of brass, and cut the bars of iron: and He will give me the treasures of darkness and hidden riches of secret places (Isaiah 45:2-3).

- I am willing and obedient, so I shall eat the best of the land (Isaiah 1:19).

- I obey and serve God, so I shall spend my days in prosperity, and my years in pleasures (Job 36:11).

- I know the grace of my Lord Jesus Christ, that though He was rich, yet for my sake He became poor, that I through His poverty might become rich (2 Corinthians 8:9).

- The wealth of sinners is laid up for me, for I am righteous in Christ (Proverbs 13:22).

- Because I am faithful, I shall abound with blessings (Proverbs 28:20).

- I delight myself in the Lord, and He shall give me the desires of my heart (Psalm 37:4).

- God is doing exceedingly abundantly above all that I ask or think, according to the power that works in me (Ephesians 3:20).

- God's divine power has given to me all things that pertain to life and godliness, through the knowledge of Him who called me by glory and virtue (2 Peter 1:3).

- I give, and it is given to me; good measure, pressed down, and shaken together, and running over, shall people give to me (Luke 6:38).

- I am not sluggish or lazy, but I imitate those who through faith and patience inherit God's promises (Hebrews 6:12).

- Jesus came that I might have life, and that I might have it more abundantly (John 10:10).

- I fear not, for it is my Father's good pleasure to give me His kingdom (Luke 12:32).

- The blessing of the Lord make me rich, and He adds no sorrow to it (Proverbs 10:22).

- Since I do not grow weary while doing good, in due season I shall reap because I do not lose heart (Galatians 6:9).

As you mediate on and recite these scriptures daily, they will transform your mind and heart to line up with God's promises and principles about abundance. They will enable your faith to grow so you can receive the outcomes God has promised.

PROVISION IS A PROCESS

REMEMBER: Even though God can send you prosperity in a moment of time, financial freedom usually does not happen overnight. For a family with serious financial problems, it could take five years or more to get completely out of debt and turn their finances around.

The basics of God's economic plan cannot be rushed. Yet the great temptation will be to rush this process. Instead, you must set your course, establish your plan, and stick to it.

However, you can definitely speed up your timeframe for financial independence by adding faith to the equation. When God is at work in your life, you don't have to carry out these steps in your own strength. If you do your part and invite Him into the equation, you can be sure He will be faithful to do His part.

My prayer for you is that God will give you a fresh and powerful revelation of the abundance available to you as you persistently follow His economic principles. Never give up! His help is here **NOW**.

Chapter 17

THRIVING AMID ECONOMIC CRISES
POSITION YOURSELF TO PROSPER

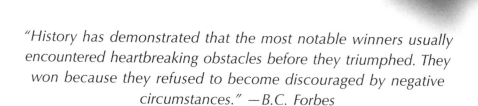

"History has demonstrated that the most notable winners usually encountered heartbreaking obstacles before they triumphed. They won because they refused to become discouraged by negative circumstances." —B.C. Forbes

"Nobody spends somebody else's money as carefully as he spends his own. Nobody uses somebody else's resources as carefully as he uses his own. So if you want efficiency and effectiveness, if you want knowledge to be properly utilized, you have to do it through private property." —Milton Friedman

ONE OF THE REASONS I wrote this book is to make people aware that there are unprecedented changes taking place in our economy. Unless we take action to position ourselves properly, these changes will have a dramatic effect on the lifestyle and legacy we leave for future generations.

If the current economic trends are allowed to continue, many of the fundamental freedoms we've taken for granted may no longer be available for our children. Most people will be unprepared unless they make adjustments and prepare themselves for the challenges ahead.

Outlined in this book are seven time-tested principles that govern wealth and long-term economic success:

THE 7 PRINCIPLES OF THE ECONOMIC DESTINY PROGRAM

- PLAN AHEAD
- PAY YOURSELF FIRST (AFTER GIVING TO GOD)
- SPEND WITHIN YOUR MEANS
- GET OUT OF DEBT
- ELIMINATE WASTE
- BECOME A WISE INVESTOR
- GIVE BACK (LEAVE A LEGACY FOR OTHERS)

By implementing these basic principles, you will be able to take control of your economic circumstances and build wealth in line with God's plan for your life, *regardless* of what happens in the economy. Storms are certain to come, but your financial house will stand firm, because it is built on a firm foundation (Matthew 7:24-27).

THE COMING ECONOMIC STORM

Honest economists are making alarming predictions, and they have had a profound impact on my view of personal and global economics. If their projections are correct, we are heading for some very difficult economic times ahead.

As a nation, we have violated many of the foundational principles that govern financial and economic success. In September and October of 2008, the U.S. was jolted by a reality check, confirming the accuracy of these economists' predictions. Because of debt and out of control spending, the U.S. economy came within days of a massive economic collapse. We are still feeling the rumblings, and now an even greater storm looms on the horizon.

As we look back over the series of events the past few years, it's clear that most of the problems we're encountering in our economy could have been avoided if we and our leaders had followed the seven principles of the Economic Destiny Program.

Even though our leaders have not openly admitted it, most of the recent problems have stemmed from debt and poor stewardship over the economic resources entrusted to their care. By spending much more than we have coming in, our nation is mortgaging the future of the next generation.

Do you know where we get the word "mortgage" from? It's derived from Latin word *mort*, meaning "death," and the old English word *gauge*, meaning "a pledge." When you put those words together, what do you have? *A death pledge!* By entering into long-term debt—whether individually or as a nation—we are literally signing "a pledge of death"! If current trends continue, many of the institutions we have depended on for retirement will no longer be available for us, our children, or our grandchildren. We can no longer depend on the government or Wall Street to protect such things as Social Security, company retirement plans, or personal investment plans.

THOMAS JEFFERSON ON THE DANGERS OF DEBT

President Thomas Jefferson recognized and warned against the consequences of personal and government debt as it relates to future generations:

Then I say, the earth belongs to each of these generations during its course, fully and in its own right. The second generation receives it clear of the debts and encumbrances of the first, the third of the second, and so on. For if the first could charge it with a debt, then the earth would belong to the dead and not to the living generation. **Then, no generation can contract debts greater than may be paid during the course of its own existence...**

The conclusion then, is, that neither the representatives of a nation [government], nor the whole nation itself assembled,

can validly engage debts beyond what they may pay in their own time (Thomas Jefferson to James Madison, 1789. ME 7:457, Papers 15:398n).

As we look at our nation's financial activities in the past 75 years, we realize that Thomas Jefferson's warning about debt is now coming to pass: massive debt is being passed on from one generation to future generations.

Because of excessive debt at the personal, corporate and national levels, we are presently experiencing much more than a typical economic downturn. Although many people continue playing by the established rules regarding savings and investments, these rules no longer apply in the current environment.

If we don't change our current economic course as a nation, we could end up being devastated by an irreversible economic storm. The present trajectory is clearly unsustainable, and many economists believe we are already past the point of no return. Despite warning signs everywhere, there might not be the political will to address the real problem: ever-growing government, which fuels ever-greater spending and debt.

In a letter to Samuel Kercheval 200 years ago, Thomas Jefferson warned that perpetual debt inevitably results in perpetual servitude:

To preserve [the] independence [of the people,] we must not let our rulers load us with perpetual debt. We must make our election between *economy and liberty,* or *profusion and servitude.* If we run into such debts whereby we must be taxed in our meat and in our drink, in our necessaries and our comforts, in our labors and our amusements, for our callings and our creeds, as the people of England are, our people, like them, must come to labor sixteen hours in the twenty-four, give the earnings of fifteen of these to the government for their debts and daily expenses, and the sixteenth being insufficient to afford us bread, we must live, as they now do, on oatmeal and potatoes, have no time to think, no means of calling the mismanagers to account, but be glad to obtain subsistence by hiring ourselves to rivet their chains on the necks of our fellow-sufferers (Thomas Jefferson to Samuel Kercheval in 1816).

Jefferson wisely noted the connection between national debt and higher taxes, a sad reality we will surely experience in the years ahead. However, Jefferson also points out that even high taxes are insufficient to bring about economic stability in a nation that is deeply in debt. The people lose their independence and liberty, ending up in "servitude" and "chains."

Evidence of this servitude is already appearing. In April 2010, the U.S. government released its first positive report on unemployment figures in more than a year, and the newscasters just breezed right though the report. This seemed very strange to me, so I looked up *who* was recently employed.

Of the new jobs created, 96% were not private sector jobs that could actually have stimulated our economy. No, out of the 245,000 new jobs created, 210,000 were IRS agents and Census workers! Government was the only institution expanding, and it was building an ever-increasing workforce to rivet chains on the citizens of this great nation.

Just as in Jefferson's statement, when people are weakened and disempowered by big government, they become hungry and will drop their morals and better judgment just to feed themselves. Their desperation will lead them to take any job they find, even if it requires them to rivet chains around their neighbors' necks.

PAST RULES DON'T APPLY

Many people are still playing by the established rules, hoping their economic circumstances will somehow improve. They have gone to school, gotten good jobs, and are doing the best they can to take care of their families. They work hard on their careers, and some own businesses. With an expectation of retiring at around age 65, they are faithfully saving and investing, and their plan is to live on Social Security and their company retirement plan (stock options, IRA, 401(k), etc.).

But few people realize the rules have changed. The near collapse of the world economy in the fall of 2008 was another sign of major problems to come. It also signaled a "changing of the guard" to a new generation of leadership. Unfortunately, this new generation has a different mindset regarding the importance of stewardship and economic accountability.

If current trends continue regarding the national debt, there will be even more drastic changes in our economy in the near future. Many of these changes are already well underway as of this writing in the summer of 2010. However, there's good news in the midst of these dangerous trends:

THOSE WHO KNOW WHAT TO EXPECT AND PROPERLY POSITION THEMSELVES CAN PROSPER REGARDLESS OF WHAT HAPPENS IN THE NATIONAL OR GLOBAL ECONOMY.

In order to prepare ourselves, there are several economic signposts we should be paying closer attention to. Look at these disturbing symptoms:

- Today it takes $1,200 to buy a single ounce of gold, when only a few years ago it took just $350.

- The dollar is getting constantly weaker and has recently hit a 14-year low against the Japanese Yen.[7]

- On November 25, 2009, *The Wall Street Journal* reported that lending from American banks had fallen to its lowest point since the government began to track those statistics.[8]

- On December 5, 2009, the FDIC shut down six more banks, which brought the total number of bank failures to 130 for the year of 2009.[9] And by the end of March 2010, 41 more banks were added to the list of closures.

The bottom line is this—the U.S. government is spending trillions more than it takes in each year.

---

7   Associated Press—Business Insider, November 25, 2009, Arbel and Erin Conroy in NY
8   *Wall Street Journal*, November 29, 2009. Damien Paletta, New York, NY
9   Associated Press, December 5, 2009, Marcy Gordon, Washington, DC

Because of poor financial stewardship, we are now a debtor nation, no longer commanding the same respect and admiration from the world community. We've become a nation in bondage to debt and credit. We operate on borrowed money, and soon the national debt will hit the point where the interest alone will be more than the nation's income.

Sadly, many Americans are following the government's lead regarding debt and overspending. Countless people strive for good credit scores, but for the wrong reason—so they can go further into debt. As a result, we are seeing millions of people facing foreclosure or bankruptcy. Many others are out of work, with very little hope for obtaining adequate employment.

On November 29, 2009, United Press International reported that there are now 20,000 new applications for food stamps *every day*. As of April 2010, Fox News reported that the national unemployment rate for college graduates was approaching 21%.

THE UNSUSTAINABLE NATIONAL DEBT

What impact is this having on our national economy? The implications are far-reaching, and they affect every aspect of our national and international financial priorities. From a spiritual perspective, we are now servants to the lenders—China, Japan, Middle Eastern countries, and other world banks that most of us don't even know the names of.

This not only has implications for our national sovereignty, but it impacts employment, housing, and our government's ability to provide basic human services. Many experts believe that if the economy continues on its current course of excessive spending and extreme debt, there is certain to be another, far worse, economic crisis. Why? Because the interest on our national debt is continuing to increase to ever-greater percentages of our gross national income.

The U.S. public debt in 2009 was 83.29% of our Gross Domestic Product (GDP). It's projected to rise to 89% of GDP by the end of

2010 and to 92.47% of GDP in 2011.[10] The annual interest on our national debt as of August 2010 is over $375 billion and is projected to reach over $500 billion by 2011.[11]

To put these numbers in perspective, the interest on our debt will soon equal about 1/3 (33%) of all the taxes collected in the U.S. In comparison, think of it this way: If your household spends 33 cents of every dollar of every paycheck just to pay the monthly interest on your debts, would you say you are living in freedom or bondage? It would be time to take immediate action to remedy the situation!

It's been a long time since the government has shown any restraint in curbing its hunger for more borrowing and spending. But the frightening economic projections are a clear warning sign that we must change our course if we want to preserve our nation's freedom and prosperity.

Although many see the troubling signs, they don't understand the urgency of preparing for what is coming. They've never considered what steps they should take to get ready for the changes ahead.

So what should we do as individuals in light of the perilous circumstances ahead? Our first priority should be to get out of debt, and this comes by reorganizing our finances according to the principles outlined in the Economic Destiny Program.

In another letter from Thomas Jefferson to Albert Gallatin in 1809, he wrote:

> I consider the fortunes of our republic as depending in an eminent degree on the extinguishment of the public debt before we engage in any war; because that done, we shall have revenue enough to improve our country in peace and defend it in war without recurring either new taxes or loans. But if the debt should once more be swelled to a formidable size, its entire discharge will be despaired of, and we shall be committed to the English career of debt, corruption and rottenness, closing

---

10   U.S. Federal Debt Chart: August 5, 2010 http://www.usgovernmentspending.com/federal_debt_chart.html

11   U.S. Bureau of the Public Debt: Treasury Direct.GOV: August 5, 2010 http://www.treasurydirect.gov/govt/reports/ir/ir_expense.htm

with revolution. The discharge of public debt, therefore, is vital to the destinies of our government.

This prophetic warning from Thomas Jefferson was written in 1809—more than 200 years ago. He warns us to stop spending and get out of debt, so we can remain in a position to defend our country from its enemies and preserve our legacy of freedom for coming generations. What a timely message this remains for our nation today.

WHAT TO EXPECT

Here are some things we can expect to happen in the near future if current trends continue:

THE U.S. ECONOMY – The government debt will continue to rise as deficit spending spirals out of control. This will be accompanied by further declines in real estate values, high unemployment, and very low savings rates. Unless there is a serious reduction in government spending, there will be a deflationary cycle in the near future. Burdened by debt, fewer people will be able to buy houses and consumer goods.

THE GLOBAL ECONOMY – As with the U.S. economy, the global economy will continue to decline. Major countries such as England, China and Japan will have their own financial difficulties that will cause them to slow down on buying U.S. treasury bonds. This will make it necessary for the U.S. to print more money to cover government obligations. The world's financial foundations will continue to weaken, and the U.S. dollar will continue to lose value. Meanwhile, other industrial economies around the world will be strained as the U.S. bond and financial markets decline.

DEFLATION AND INFLATION – If current trends continue during the next 5 to 10 years, deflation will end and inflation will take off. Hyperinflation—and rapidly increasing prices—will come because of government overspending and the increase of "printing press money."

YOUR
Economic Destiny

HEALTHCARE – Healthcare costs will continue to increase even with the passage of the healthcare overhaul bill in 2010. As more people are added to Medicare and Medicaid, a greater cost burden will be added to the overall healthcare system. The cost will increase, and the quality and availability of services will decline.

HOUSING – Sales will continue to decline over a period of time for both new and old houses. This will be primarily caused by stagnation in the economy and a decrease in home buying among the Baby Boomers. As a result of these demographic trends, there will be added strain on the housing market, Social Security and Medicare. Already, Social Security is operating as a $10 trillion unfunded liability, and it's projected to run out of money before 2020 unless drastic changes are made.

EMPLOYMENT – Unemployment will rise above 10% nationwide and more than 20% in some urban communities. Bankruptcies will continue to increase as more companies are forced to lay off their employees. Pressure will continue in the housing market because of jobs lost. Since 70% of the American people have no savings, a sudden loss of income will be devastating.

WALL STREET – Although you can expect some short-term gains in the stock market, most of the long-term fundamentals are negative. If current trends continue, the stock market will fluctuate up and down, but could ultimately drop to 5,000 or even lower.

CREDIT MARKETS – Banks, credit card companies, and lending institutions will tighten their credit. They will face another major crisis because of defaults on credit cards and commercial loans. Interest rates on your credit cards will increase, and your credit limits will decrease. The tightening credit will cause discretionary spending on consumer goods to decrease, which will put more downward pressure on corporate earnings and stocks.

INFLATION – If the government does not get spending under control, our nation's credit rating will drop, which will dramatically increase our cost of borrowing money. As China and other countries reduce their holdings of U.S. bonds, our government will be forced to print more money, causing hyperinflation and a further strain on the dollar. Gas prices will increase to expected highs of $5.00 to $7.00, and this will create a ripple effect of high prices for food and other goods.

TAX INCREASES – Taxes and fees of every kind will increase. Some of these tax hikes will be obvious, but others will be virtually hidden in "the cost of doing business."

EMERGENCY FOOD SUPPLIES – It's very possible that many areas of the country will face natural disasters or terrorist attacks that will limit people's access to vital resources such as electricity, food, water and medical supplies. Be prepared! Store up food, water and other supplies *before* disasters strike. Many organizations such as the American Red Cross recommend maintaining enough food and water for your family to last a period of at least two weeks. This is the very minimum you need. I suggest 6 months to one year would be a more realistic goal so you can go beyond helping your own family and position yourself to be a blessing to your neighbors.

ACTION STEPS FOR THE COMING STORM

It's one thing to realize an economic storm is coming, and another thing to take the necessary steps to prepare for it. So what can you do to get ready for the financial crises ahead?

ACTION STEP #1: GET OUT OF DEBT.

Avoid taking on any new debt. If you have no house payment, car notes, or other debts, you'll be able to live above most economic situations. Be content with what you have unless you can pay cash, but make it your priority to build a cash reserve. Become a good steward (manager) over the things God has already entrusted to your care. Learn frugality, and do what you can to return to the simple life. (Visit **www.youreconomicdestiny.org** for more information.)

ACTION STEP #2: INCREASE YOUR SAVINGS.

Regardless of economic conditions or the current financial situation you're in, start to establish your surplus (reserve fund). Make this a priority. Pay yourself first after God, then consider all of your other bills later. Force everything else around this priority.

ACTION STEP #3: ELIMINATE AUTOMOBILE DEBT.

Set a priority to eliminate all car payments. Be content with your existing car unless you can pay cash or use the INFINITE BANKING CONCEPT plan to borrow money from yourself. If you have upside down auto debt, you should consider selling your car at a loss in order to eliminate your monthly payments. Consider purchasing a car that is two or three years old, and pay cash for it. **REMEMBER:** Your goal is to own your car free and clear, with no loans or monthly payments. The money you save can be used to build your reserve fund or YOUR IBC PLAN.

ACTION STEP #4: INCREASE YOUR MEDICAL DEDUCTIBLES.

Consider using the IBC policy in place of a health savings account (HSA), and use this to increase your personal deductibles. This will help you decrease the cost of your medical expenses.

ACTION STEP #5: ELIMINATE YOUR MORTGAGE.

Your objective in the Economic Destiny Program is to own your home free and clear, even if you have to downsize. Home prices will continue to drop in many areas, so make your decisions accordingly.

Live within your means. Purchase a home based on genuine need and what you truly can afford. Visit **www.youreconomicdestiny.org** for information on how you can pay off your mortgage in just 5 to 7 years or less.

ACTION STEP #6: EXPECT THE BEST BUT PREPARE FOR THE WORST.

Take time to realistically assess what would happen if you lost your job or had a significant drop in income. You need an action plan for such scenarios, and getting out of debt is the essential first step.

ACTION STEP #7: SEEK SAFE INVESTMENTS.

Remember that there's a difference between saving and investing. Reduce your risk of loss by transferring your savings accounts away from traditional Wall Street investments such as mutual funds, IRAs and 401(k)s. Instead, consider safer investments such as cash-value life insurance plans, homeownership (free and clear), gold, silver, etc.

ACTION STEP #8: CREATE AN EMERGENCY SUPPLY OF FOOD AND WATER.

Take time now to prepare an emergency food and water supply so you can provide for your family and others in a time of crisis. Focus on food your family eats on a regular basis, and develop a system for rotating that stored food based on the expiration dates on the packaging. Most dried and canned foods will last up to six months, but check the dates on the packaging. Freeze-dried foods and dehydrated foods can last over 25 years and will maintain their vital nutrients. Every time you empty a plastic carton of milk, rinse it out and fill it with tap water for storage.

FINDING A REFUGE FROM THE STORMS

When considering how we should position ourselves for the coming economic storm, it's important to mention again the vital role that faith must play in our lives. The Biblical writers frequently mention God's amazing protection in times of trouble. Yes, storms will come, but we can safely withstand them if our lives are built upon Christ, the Rock (Matthew 7:24-27).

In Isaiah 4:5-6 (NIV), we're promised that God will give us a "canopy" to protect us from life's storms: "It will be a shelter and shade from the heat of the day, and a refuge and hiding place from the storm and rain" (Isaiah 4:5-6). No matter what challenges you face today—in your finances or other aspects of your life—the Lord wants to be your "refuge and hiding place."

Take a few minutes to meditate on the wonderful promises in Psalm 91 about God's desire to keep you safe, even when there's danger all around you:

> He who dwells in the secret place of the Most High
> Shall abide under the shadow of the Almighty.
> I will say of the LORD, "He is my refuge and my fortress;
> My God, in Him I will trust."
> Surely He shall deliver you from the snare of the fowler
> And from the perilous pestilence.
> He shall cover you with His feathers,
> And under His wings you shall take refuge;
> His truth shall be your shield and buckler.
> You shall not be afraid of the terror by night,
> Nor of the arrow that flies by day,
> Nor of the pestilence that walks in darkness,
> Nor of the destruction that lays waste at noonday.
> A thousand may fall at your side,
> And ten thousand at your right hand;
> But it shall not come near you.
> Only with your eyes shall you look,
> And see the reward of the wicked.

Because you have made the LORD**, who is my refuge,**
Even the Most High, your dwelling place,
No evil shall befall you,
Nor shall any plague come near your dwelling;
For He shall give His angels charge over you,
To keep you in all your ways.
In their hands they shall bear you up,
Lest you dash your foot against a stone.
You shall tread upon the lion and the cobra,
The young lion and the serpent you shall trample underfoot.
"Because he has set his love upon Me, therefore I will deliver him;
I will set him on high, because he has known My name.
He shall call upon Me, and I will answer him;
I will be with him in trouble;
I will deliver him and honor him.
With long life I will satisfy him,
And show him My salvation."

No matter what turmoil may emerge on the world's financial stage, we don't need to be afraid. Though the storms may rage, He will be our refuge and fortress.

And the key to overcoming fear is simply this: Knowing that He is with us!

Fear not, for I am with you;
Be not dismayed, for I am your God.
I will strengthen you,
Yes, I will help you,
I will uphold you with My righteous right hand (Isaiah 41:10).

BLESSING OTHERS EVEN IN TOUGH TIMES

Earlier in the book, I shared how God blessed a poor widow when she took a step of faith to feed the prophet Elijah (1 Kings 17:8-16). Never forget that God wants to bless you so that you can BE a blessing to others. Even in a time of famine, this poor widow was able to reach out her hand in compassion to Elijah. As a result,

God abundantly met her needs.

This is God's plan for you as well. As you position yourself under His divine canopy of protection and provision, He will mightily use you to provide for others.

Think about it: Overflowing abundance is available even in a time of famine and economic crisis. What an incredible testimony this will be to a watching world!

WE'VE ONLY JUST BEGUN
THIS IS NOT THE END,
BUT JUST A NEW BEGINNING

THERE'S A REASON WHY I've saved the following word of encouragement and buried it deep in the back of this book:

THIS IS A MESSAGE WRITTEN ONLY FOR
YOU WHO ARE HUNGRY FOR TRUTH!

You wouldn't have continued on this journey with me if you didn't have a sincere desire to transform your economic destiny. I acknowledge the greatness of your quest, your courage and your fortitude. This final message has already been a repeated theme throughout the book, sometimes written in bold print and sometimes only between the lines.

Here it is one more time:

IF YOU ARE GOING TO REACH YOUR INTENDED PURPOSE
FOR LIVING, YOU MUST SEEK WISDOM AND KNOWLEDGE
FROM THE ONE WHO CREATED YOU AND NOW GIVES
YOU EVERY BREATH YOU BREATHE.

If you're going to live a life of freedom and abundance instead of scarcity and lack, then you must be willing to lay aside the fool's gold you've been trained to pursue. Instead, you must make it your supreme ambition to find the solid Gold that was intended for you since the beginning of time.

GET WISDOM!

King Solomon, the richest man who has ever lived, described it this way:

> **Get wisdom! Get understanding!**
> **Do not forget, nor turn away from the words of my mouth.**
> **Do not forsake her, and she will preserve you;**
> **Love her, and she will keep you.**
> **Wisdom is the principal thing;**
> **Therefore get wisdom.**
> **And in all your getting, get understanding.**
> **Exalt her, and she will promote you;**
> **She will bring you honor, when you embrace her.**
> **She will place on your head an ornament of grace;**
> **A crown of glory she will deliver to you...**
> **When you walk, your steps will not be hindered,**
> **And when you run, you will not stumble.**
> **Take firm hold of instruction, do not let go;**
> **Keep her, for she is your life (Proverbs 4:5-13).**

> **Receive my instruction, and not silver,**
> **And knowledge rather than choice gold;**
> **For wisdom is better than rubies,**
> **And all the things one may desire cannot be compared with her**
> **(Proverbs 8:10-11).**

Solomon recognized that his ultimate security was not in the amount of his silver and gold, but rather in his relationship with God and his commitment to walk in God's wisdom.

The same is true for you. In this book, I've sought to point you to powerful keys for transforming your economic destiny. But as important as that is, God has an even higher purpose: He wants to also transform your *eternal* destiny!

Yes, the Lord wants to give you a "money makeover," but He doesn't want to stop there…He wants to give you a *TOTAL* makeover. That will come as you come into a personal relationship with Him, seek His wisdom, and have your mind renewed by His Word (Romans 12:2).

Are you ready to acknowledge God as the owner of everything and the source of all you need? Are you ready to trust Him to show you His will for your life?

God's will for you is found in His Word. It's as simple as this: His will is His Word. While I've sought to unveil what the Bible says about your intended destiny, I don't want you to take my word for it. You need to spend time discovering God's truth for yourself—and when you find the truth, you can be certain it will *set you free*! (John 8:32)

A GOLDEN RULE OF FINANCE

I want to leave you with a foundational Golden Rule of Finance:

YOU WERE DESIGNED BY YOUR CREATOR TO OPERATE AS A FREE CITIZEN, IN A FREE MARKET AND UNDER NO ONE ELSE'S CONTROL. HE DESIGNED YOU TO LOOK TO HIM ALONE AS YOUR PROVIDER!

This clearly sounds like a radical idea in today's world. Aren't we to look to Wall Street, our local banks, or the government for our security and prosperity?

NO! The world's financial systems are built upon false prosperity and fool's gold. They're fueled by fear and scarcity instead surplus and abundance. It's crucial that we understand this unpleasant truth if we going to raise up the next generation in a free society where they can reach their unlimited potential and experience the life they were created for.

The world's economic system is designed to have you look to it for your supply, your welfare and your income. As a result, it determines the value of your labor, your resources and your property. The system has seized "command and control" over our lives, but most of us no longer even question our position of servitude. We're too busy just striving to provide the essentials for our families.

The system has created a boom and bust economy that destroys our lives and robs us of our intended nest egg. Taking a page right out of Genesis 1 (where God says, "Let there be light!"), the central bankers are arrogantly saying, "Let there be money!" How can this turn out well? Unless their course is reversed, the certain outcome will be more and more central control over you, your business and your family.

You may say, "I don't really understand what are you're talking about, Jeff." Well, stay with me just another few minutes.

You need to grasp a powerful truth that has critical impact on your economic destiny. Look at the facts about how your hard-earned wealth has been stolen by inflation and deflation:

- The U.S. dollar has fallen in value by 95% over the past 100 years.

- In contrast, an ounce of gold 100 years ago holds the exact same purchasing power today.

- A hundred years ago, an ounce of gold would buy a pair of shoes, a belt, a nice suit, a nice dinner out with the family, and groceries for a week. Today, that same ounce of gold will *still* buy you a pair of shoes, a belt, a nice suit, a nice dinner out with the family, and groceries for a week.

- Meanwhile, dollars produced by the central banking monetary system today have only 5% of their purchasing power. Instead of the long list of items you could purchase with your gold, your dollars would be lucky to even buy you a nice dinner out with your family!

WHO OWNS THE GOLD?

Perhaps you've heard an old financial maxim that says…

"HE WHO OWNS THE GOLD MAKES THE RULES!"

From the beginning of time, God has made it clear that *He* owns the silver and the gold (Haggai 2:8), and He distributes it to whoever manages it well (Mathew 25:29). God also says He wants to give His people wisdom to find the gold, mine the gold, and use it to bless their lives and the lives of others.

Yet today there is increasing evidence that our money supply and free market system are under the control of powerful central bankers. The value of goods is no longer based on something of intrinsic value (such as gold or silver). This is in direct opposition to the natural monetary system God instituted from the beginning of time.

Instead of being content with their Constitutional powers, politicians have joined with bankers in coveting the wealth of God's free people and devising plans to take central control. Together, they've conspired to sidestep God's economic system. In essence, the politicians and central bankers have said:

"We want more 'gold' than God has given us, so we're going to create our own money supply and print as much as we like. That way, we can become our own provider. By controlling the distribution and value of people's wealth, we can ultimately control the people and their destiny for generations to come. They will serve us! He who owns the gold makes the rules!"

GOD IS STILL ON THE THRONE

I apologize if this sounds like too much doom and gloom—that is not my intention. I want you to have your eyes wide open to the geopolitical forces at work against your financial prosperity. But much MORE than that, I want you to remember who is *really* in control. Just because influential people have been trying to take the place of God, that doesn't mean His economic system is no longer in effect for those who acknowledge it, implement its principles, and tap into its blessings.

God hasn't relinquished control of the universe to the politicians and the bankers! None of the financial tsunamis of recent years have caught Him off guard. He's still on the throne! (See Revelation 4:1-2.)

So how does God respond when political or economic turmoil shakes the nations? Psalm 2:1-4 gives us a helpful glimpse at the heavenly perspective:

> **Why do the nations rage,**
> **And the people plot a vain thing?**
> **The kings of the earth set themselves,**
> **And the rulers take counsel together,**
> **Against the LORD and against His Anointed, saying,**
> **"Let us break Their bonds in pieces**
> **And cast away Their cords from us."**
> **He who sits in the heavens shall laugh;**
> **The Lord shall hold them in derision.**

Yes, the nations will rage. Yes, "kings" (political and financial leaders) will plot against God's purposes and try to cast off His authority. But in the midst of it all, God merely sits on His throne and laughs at their arrogance. His purposes *will* be established for us as His people, regardless of every obstacle set in our way.

FINDING A SECURE ECONOMIC DESTINY

The good news is that your personal economic destiny doesn't have to be dependent on the ups and downs of Wall Street, the financial markets, or even the American government. But you must take steps now—in both your *beliefs* and your *actions*—to find the only source of security that will never let you down.

The apostle Paul says this about the One you can always depend upon: "Whoever believes in *Him* will not be disappointed" (Romans 10:11 NASB). But the converse is also true: If you put your reliance on people, systems or investments *other than* the Lord, you sure **WILL** be disappointed!

If you will acknowledge God as your source, He will show you that the economic system of His kingdom is eternal and full of abundance. He will unlock your financial prison cell, break your chains of debt, and bring down the walls that have enslaved you to a life of poverty, scarcity and servitude. He will set you free from the disempowerment and bondage that comes from depending on others as your source—especially the government's entitlement systems.

If you continue to look to something or someone other than your Creator to provide for you, you'll be like a person who foolishly trades their diamonds for cubic zirconias. You are smarter and wiser than that! And how do I claim to know this about you? Because I know the One who created you and fashioned you to be free and reach your intended destiny. His treasures are unlimited in quantity and unmatched in quality, and they cannot be compared to what any man, government, or institution could ever provide for you.

PRESERVING LIBERTY

Our time together must now come to a fork in the road. I must continue my efforts to present this message to as many as will listen, and you must choose which direction you will go. In parting, I will leave you with a brief personal reflection.

I was born in the small town of Bothell, Washington, located in the beautiful Pacific Northwest in the United States of America. Although I had no choice in the matter of where I was born and raised, I'm proud of my heritage. I am proud to be an American, and I am blessed and honored to share in the many freedoms that come with citizenship in this great nation.

I recognize my citizenship as a gift granted by divine purpose, and yet I also am aware of the stewardship and responsibility attached to this gift. I am not too spoiled, numb or blinded by the rich beauty of my inheritance to see that my freedoms came with a hefty price—a price I did not pay, with sacrifices I did not personally make.

As a citizen of this great sovereign nation, I have a responsibility to learn, understand, protect and uphold our Constitutional foundations. I must be willing to protect those freedoms won by courageous men and women I did not know and who did not know me. Instead of having their own interests at heart, they sought to win and preserve liberty for you and me and the generations to come.

Today you have freedom to sit out in the open air and hold the Bible or this book in your hand, without fear of consequences. Yes, the dreams and sacrifices of our forefathers were not in vain but continue to impact and bless our lives today.

Remember that freedom's work is not done—nor is it *ever* done. Each new generation must bear the torch of liberty and pass it on to future generations. Today the dream and destiny of freedom rests upon the shoulders of you and me.

Be vigilant, diligent and always on guard, lest you become lulled to sleep due to conveniences, luxuries and the many freedoms we can so easily take for granted. Don't be caught waking up someday to a world of bondage, where your independence has been exchanged for dependence on someone or something other than your Creator.

CHOOSE WISELY

You had opportunities to put this book down many pages ago. You could have set it on the shelf, thrown it in the garbage, or simply rejected its message as being the opinion of only one man.

But now is the hard part. You have another choice to make. Will you take hold of the book's message and begin to integrate its principles into your life? Will you not only believe its truths, but devise a plan to act upon them? The choice is yours and always will be yours—so choose wisely.

Before you make this pivotal decision, I encourage you to think—I mean *really* think—about what you've read. Decide only after you have meditated on, examined and imagined for yourself the freedom, clarity and economic destiny that can be yours. Make sure you are truly ready to abandon the alternative paths, which lead only to worry, lack, risk, fear, scarcity and, ultimately, to serfdom.

Of course, you can keep doing what others do. But if everyone else is on the right path, why aren't they happy, healthy, wealthy, secure, and blessed with enough abundance to *be* a blessing to others?

AND REMEMBER: If you don't make a choice for yourself and act now, it's inevitable that your economic choices will simply be made for you. You will continue drifting down the bleak current called the path of least resistance.

There really are just two paths you can go from here. You can continue imitating what the masses do—leading to powerlessness, scarcity, deprivation and dependence on others. Or you can begin your journey to a new economic destiny. Instead of being dependent on others, you can have a destiny of financial independence, because you're only dependent on the One who owns it all!

Until we meet, I'll leave you with this ancient Hebrew blessing:

The LORD bless you and keep you;

The LORD make His face shine upon you,

And be gracious to you;

The LORD lift up His countenance upon you,

And give you peace (Numbers 6:24-26).

God Bless You!

Jeff Mendenhall

DISCLAIMER:

INSURANCE DISCLAIMER

THE ILLUSTRATIONS IN THIS BOOK ARE FOR EDUCATIONAL PURPOSES ONLY. They are not intended to represent or guarantee a particular result. They are not intended to provide legal, tax, insurance, investment, financial, accounting, or other professional advice or services. The illustrations contained within this book do not seek to represent or promote a particular insurance company, agent, or policy. Results differ state by state, insurance company, agent, and riders due to specific contractual design requirements, performance of company and relevant state laws.

Dividends illustrated are not guaranteed and may be declared annually by the insurance company's board of directors. The figures depending on dividends are based on the non-guaranteed dividend scale and are not guaranteed. Illustrations provided in this book assume that the currently illustrated non-guaranteed elements, including dividends, will continue unchanged for all years shown, but the actual results may be more favorable than illustrated or less favorable than illustrated as dividends are declared year by year based on the future performance of the company and other factors calculated by the board of directors. For an accurate, personalized illustration, please see an insurance professional who is competent to compose a proper illustration.

Loans on participating whole life policies are typically income tax free while the policy remains in force, provided that the policy is not considered a MEC modified endowment contract. The policies, as shown, will not become a MEC. The term MEC is designated under federal tax law. If a policy becomes a MEC, then any surrenders, withdrawals, or policy loans will be taxed less favorably than for a non-MEC.

The illustrations shown in this book illustrate one or more paid up additional payments after years 5-10 that exceed the basic base and PUA policy premium. The insured may need to provide evidence of insurability before the insurance company accepts payments in excess of this limit. The insurance products illustrated within this book may not be available in your state or from your preferred insurance provider. Premiums must be paid if the policy is to remain in force, unless designed otherwise. The policy as illustrated may not be available to all applicants, and premiums may differ based on health qualifications.